the Building Blocks
of Positive Parenting

INCLUDES 17 OF THE MOST COMMON CHILDHOOD DISORDERS

the Building Blocks of Positive Parenting

SPECIFIC STRATEGIES AND SKILLS ALL PARENTS NEED!

BARBARA ROBA, ED.M, CAS, LMHC

TATE PUBLISHING
AND ENTERPRISES, LLC

Published by Tate Publishing & Enterprises, LLC
127 E. Trade Center Terrace | Mustang, Oklahoma 73064 USA
1.888.361.9473 | www.tatepublishing.com

Tate Publishing is committed to excellence in the publishing industry. The company reflects the philosophy established by the founders, based on Psalm 68:11,
"The Lord gave the word and great was the company of those who published it."

Book design copyright © 2015 by Tate Publishing, LLC. All rights reserved.
Cover design by Junriel Boquecosa
Interior design by Joana Quilantang

Published in the United States of America

ISBN: 978-1-63306-595-6
Family & Relationships / Children with Special Needs
14.12.08

Practical and Positive Behavior Interventions
For Parents and Teachers

The purpose of parenting is to produce well-adjusted individuals who will be self-sufficient and who will make a positive contribution to the world.

The very best way to ensure that happens is to provide our children with unconditional

love,

support,

patience,

guidance,

tolerance, and

acceptance.

Congratulations! You have the best job in the world: being a parent! You can help to mold our planet's future by supporting your children along their journey to adulthood.

Their future rests in your loving hands.

To God, my greatest source of strength and guidance.
To my three boys. Because of you, all of this is possible.
To all the children of the world, each of you are
a blessing. May that fact be recognized.

Along the parenting path, many obstacles will arise.
Rest easy. You have come to the right place for answers.

Contents

Introduction

Read This First!

Goldmine! You hold in your hands the most comprehensive and easy-to-use collection of parenting strategies available. Wait! It gets better! The majority of the interventions in this book can be put into place today. Hope now has a plan!

Keep reading and you will find the most common childhood behavior problems paired with effective interventions to get your family back on track and to keep them there.

This book paired with online parenting support found at behaviorcorner.com is the cornerstone to raising your children to be their very best.

No one has ever said that parenting is easy. As a matter of fact, I have heard many people agree with the old adage "It takes a village to raise a child." Do you know why that is? Let me tell you.

My name is Barb Roba, and I am a licensed mental health counselor, a certified life coach, a school counselor, and most importantly, I am a parent.

In all my years working with children and raising my own, I stand firm in the belief that children need many positive and supportive people in their lives to show them how to interact within society—hence, the necessity of that village to raise a child.

If I may, I would like to make a modification to this age-old saying so that it reads, "It takes a positive, consistent, and supportive village to raise a respectful, well-rounded child." There, we just created a new statement to live by. Congratulations!

Throughout this book, you will come across many references to *positivity*, *consistency*, and *support*. Not only do these traits need to come from others in your children's life, they most importantly need to come from you—the parent.

Being a parent with these traits is really the greatest gift you can give to your children. Just a few benefits that you and your family will reap from these parenting traits include the following:

- Children quickly learn how to behave.
- Children learn how to live up to your expectations.
- Children have a confidence in knowing where the boundaries lie.
- Children have a greater chance of turning out to be successful members of society.

Of course, all children test the limits in an attempt to figure out which expectations are hard and fast rules and which they are allowed to bend. Use your discretion here, and be ready to give explanations of any "gray areas" that life throws our way. Doing this will help your children to understand the exceptions to the rules of life.

Remember that children are most stable, responsible, respectful, loving, and have the strongest bond with those who lovingly hold them accountable. The secrets to achieving this await you in the pages that follow.

The real magic occurs when regular, positive acknowledgement prevents misbehavior altogether.

Kudos to you for picking this book to make your life and the lives of those in your home happier by creating respectful, responsible, and grateful behavior.

Before you get started in looking for solutions to your exact problem, I urge you to read the following four chapters. They contain spot-on parenting advice and the secrets to raising kids that apply to *all* areas of development and need.

Enjoy!

Reality

A word on perfect: There is no perfect parent. There is no perfect child. There is no perfect way to raise your children. Perfect does not exist.

The best way to do "perfect" is to keep your children's best interests in mind. To do so, start by thinking. Think about your parenting style. Think about the ways in which you react to your children. Think about the consequences you use.

Reading through these introductory chapters and then on to your particular chapters of need, you will stumble upon an enormous amount of ideas and advice.

However, at this moment, the only advice you need is: *go slow*. You and your children will need time to practice, make changes, and get used to this new and improved lifestyle.

Get a good handle on the foundations to successful parenting presented in the first few chapters. Once they are comfortably in place, start to add a strategy or two from the list of your greatest need. For example, if your child struggles with anxiety, paying attention, and is sometimes argumentative, your best bet is to work toward addressing their anxiety as this is the primary issue that is impacting their overall functioning. In other words, anxiety is the greatest need and should be focused upon first.

Beware: the best intentions don't always go as planned. You and I are human. We let our emotions get the best of us sometimes. Our children are masters at pushing our buttons, and we don't always do and say what is most beneficial in the heat of the moment. I get it. I've been there, and I continue to work on always getting better.

Give yourself a break if your idea to remain calm and your resolution to not engage in verbal battling goes right out the window. Although I don't recommend you making a habit of this, it can be a good lesson for your children to see that you too are not perfect. Your behavior should be spoken about once everyone is calm so that your children can gain an understanding of not only their behavior but yours as well.

It is okay to make mistakes. Let me tell you why.

Our children learn from us. We are the primary models in their lives. When we admit that we made a mistake and talk about what we will do differently next time, it builds respect and teaches our children how to take responsibility for their actions.

Do your best to use the following building blocks of positive parenting. Stick to it, tweak as you go, and always remember that tomorrow is a new day.

Must-Know Parenting Strategies

The handbook that you always wished you had begins right here, right now.

At the cornerstone of parenting there are several things to keep in mind when raising your children. These "must-know" items are separated into the following categories:

1. *Foundational Skills*: Are you looking for a magic wand to improve your relationship with your children? Perhaps you are looking to improve their behavior, or are simply reading to learn how to improve an already good situation. Whatever the reason, enjoy my no-nonsense look at how the choices you make in holding your children accountable for their actions can work in everyone's favor.

2. *Communication*: The way in which you interact with your children in verbal (the words you use) and nonverbal ways (body language and actions) is extremely powerful.

3. *Behavior*: The way in which we all choose to behave is our attempt to get the things we need and want. Your children are no exception to this fact. Take a look at what might be the driving force behind your children's behavior and what you can do about it.

4. *Intervention*: When is the best time to intervene in your child's behavior? The answer may surprise you and can be found in the intervention section toward the end of this chapter.

Foundational Skills

Having a Solid Foundation

Success is found after one takes many small steps in the right direction. Having a solid foundation in any situation is key to finding this success. Your home needs a solid foundation on which to stay standing. Your car needs a solid foundation on which to keep you safe. Your relationships need a solid foundation on which to trust one another.

A strong foundation is the cornerstone in having a positive relationship with your children. From this foundation, your children will be able to grow into responsible adults. You will both be very proud!

A very large part of this is taking a positive discipline approach with your children. Ways to do this are described below:

- Do as you say you will do every time. If you tell your children that you will play baseball with them after dinner, do so. If you tell your children that you will not gossip about others and you want them to do the same, make sure you don't gossip.

    If you do as you say each and every time, your children will trust you, know that they can rely on you, and will learn from your examples.

- Consistency, consistency, consistency! Children are masters at figuring out if our words match our actions.

    You must show consistency between your words and actions—every time. If your words do no match your actions, you children will not take you seriously. As a result, your words will be ignored. They will interpret your inconsistency as permission to dismiss your attempts at discipline along with dismissing the requests that you make of them. Children base their beliefs and actions on what they see.

If you are in a situation with your children where your words are being ignored, start now by matching your words and actions. When you tell your children they will go to time-out for not listening the first time a request is made, send them to time-out if they choose not to listen. If you end up repeating your request until you get frustrated and finally send them to time-out, your children learn that in reality they don't have to listen to you the first time. Even though you told them that they do, your actions did not support your words. They now know that they can ignore your request for the first few times and not suffer any consequences. Yikes!

The good news here is if you provide your children with consistency, they will begin to take your words seriously. Remember that it is normal for children to test these limits. Be patient and stand strong. It will pay off for you and your children. I promise!

• Consistently (if you haven't figured it out yet, this word is about to become your new best friend) give attention to your children's positive behavior. This includes praising their efforts and small accomplishments made toward positive behaviors. Not only am I telling you to give consistent consequences, but I am also telling you to give consistent praise. These two vital components will result in behavioral success. *Giving regular praise and rewards is the more important of the two.*

Look at your children and give them praise right now. Go ahead, I'll wait.

Make this a regular habit each and every day. Even if your children do not respond, keep praising. They are listening.

See me?
I am here to give you essential pieces of parenting wisdom. My Counselor's Corner boxes are directly related to surrounding text to give you even more must-have knowledge.
Look for me to reach your goals even faster!

Counselor's Corner
Praise to the rescue

✓ "You are so helpful. Thank you for cleaning up after dinner."
✓ "I see you used your best handwriting on your homework. Your effort makes me proud."
✓ "You make me happy that you did what I said to do the first time. You are doing a fantastic job listening today."
✓ "I noticed that you stood up for the new kid while standing outside of school today. That was a brave and responsible choice."

- When telling your children to do something, use a *clear* and *simple* (you'll be hearing these two words a lot too, so pay attention) message.

  ° Start your request with, "Please go to…" or "I need you to…"
  ° Never say things like, "It would be nice if you…" or "Could you…"
  ° Never ever end a request with the word "okay." "Please empty the dishwasher, okay?" is not a request; it is asking your children if it is okay with them if they empty the dishwasher. I'm sure you see the problem here.

- If you bend the rules and/or make excuses for your children's behavior, their manipulation and misbehavior will continue. Refer to the above bullets and stick to it!
- In order to change your children's behavior for the better, the consistent use of a positive behavior modification

program (see the behavior section in this chapter and appendix A) along with clear and specific boundaries will help make the change happen more quickly.

Counselor's Corner
Will I have to use behavior plans forever?

Wow...forever is a long time! No, behavior plans are not life-long. Phew!

Behavior plans are meant to teach children right from wrong while building in incentives to do so. When your child is part of the creation of a plan and when it is used consistently, they will respond by meeting their goals. After a few weeks of this happening, you can begin phasing out the current plan by using a long-term plan that increases the amount of time that exists between following expectations and rewards received. Eventually this can be phased out too.

However, you need to continue to verbally acknowledge them at every opportunity. This does us all good!

- Take the time to teach your children the skills that you expect of them. Once these skills are learned, highly encourage your children to continue using them regularly by being a positive example. Negative consequences can be issued for failure to use these skills only *after* they have been learned, practiced, and used by your children.

Helpful steps to take in this process include the following:

1. Give direct instruction of the desired skills.
2. Demonstrate how to use the skills.
3. Practice the skills with your children by role-playing and then using them in real-life settings.
4. Give feedback to your children first on what parts they were successful in and then what they could do to further improve.
5. Remember that learning skills is lifelong. Refine and continue to build desired skills with your children.

Question: Why should negative consequences be given only after understanding is mastered?

Answer: It would be unfair and very frustrating for your children to receive a negative consequence for something that they do not understand or lack the ability to do. Your job is to make sure your children are able to be successful with the expected skills prior to talking about and using consequences for failure to follow through.

Lucky for you, I have just given you all the steps needed to be successful! Have at it!

- Give your children plenty of consistent structure and boundaries. This is not me just giving you more advice—this is something that you *must* do! There are no gray areas and no exceptions with this one.

  When your children have your loving support to stay within established boundaries, they will experience success and feel proud. This is a stepping stone in teaching them how to be responsible and how to make positive decisions on their own. As a result, your children continue to mature and feel confidently in control of their decision-making abilities.

- Give your children clear and specific limits. "No snack one hour before dinner" and "Keep your hands, feet, and body to yourself" are clear and specific limits that your children will understand. Children crave limits and boundaries in their life. They need to know what they are and are not able to do. Limits help them to independently explore what is appropriate in life and what is not.

  Some parents are afraid of giving their children too many limits for fear that their children will be mad at them. If you are one of those parents, I've got news for you—children want limits. Not only do they want limits, they want you to enforce them consistently! They feel most comfortable with having limits because they know what you and others expect of them.

Step up and do your job by enforcing those limits!

Speaking of your job, your title is "parent." Let me say that again. Your job is to be a parent. Your job is not to be your children's friend. It is to be their parent. If you end up being friends, great! However, this perk comes later in life as an added bonus to being a parent first.

> ### Counselor's Corner
> **Parent vs. Friend**
>
> 'Parents' raise kids who are:
> - ✓ Responsible
> - ✓ Empathetic
> - ✓ Respectful
> - ✓ Grateful
> - ✓ Motivated
>
> 'Friends' raise kids who:
> - • Break the rules
> - • Engage in risky behaviors
> - • Show little respect for others
> - • Take things for granted

It is your responsibility to mold your children's decision-making ability through setting limits and boundaries. When you do this, it is common to see your children's drive for independence and rebellion increase, especially in adolescence. To counter this, stand up and do the right thing by being the parent who consistently recognizes their children's positive choices along with delivering consistent negative consequences when warranted. Your children will have deeper respect for you when you do. The younger your children are when you begin this, the easier time you will have raising them as they get older.

Trust me on this one, be a parent first and a friend second. You can't go wrong.

- Speaking of limits, children test limits all the time. This is the exploring that I mentioned above. Being allowed to explore the limits of life and obtaining consistent results from caregivers are the main interventions that develop your children into the adults they will become. Did you catch that? A main intervention—jackpot!

Expect limit testing. React to it in the same manner each time: give only one reminder, provide a consequence, plan for the future, and move on. See the consequences chapter for more information.

The wonderful news is that research shows that children who are raised with firm, consistent limits display less behavioral concerns. These children are more likely to follow the rules because they completely understand what is expected of them.

Of special note: Children who are determined to do things their way will require a lot of evidence that your words and actions match. They need to hear and see you handle situations consistently over and over again before change will take place. Whatever you do, don't give up and don't give in.

Praising your children's positive choices along with holding them accountable for their negative choices are both extremely powerful tools. This is especially true when you are looking for that magic wand that will mold your children into respectful, responsible, and successful individuals.

You have the power! Use it in the most loving and productive way possible. The way in which you deliver these messages of praise and accountability have a direct impact on the outcome of your interventions. (Another jackpot moment—if you were paying attention you now know that the delivery of your interventions is extremely important.)

Positive Discipline

Positive discipline demands positive parenting and respect from you when interacting with your child. The basic premise here is to teach your children. This teaching occurs when your children observe how you react to them, how you go about solving problems, and whether praise and discipline is directly related to their actions.

Discipline versus Punishment

Discipline

☐ Discipline happens over time to help children hear, see, and perform appropriate behaviors.

☐ Discipline teaches children right from wrong in loving, patient, caring, and positive ways.

☐ Discipline helps to improve children's self-esteem and sense of belonging to their family and to this world by giving them opportunities to experience success.

☐ Discipline gives positive reinforcement for all the right choices children make.

☐ Parents who use discipline take the time to talk with their children, to answer their questions, to show them right from wrong, and allow for compromise.

In what ways are you using discipline to raise your children? Check off the boxes that apply to your parenting style. Once done, take a minute to reflect upon what you can improve. Remember, there is no such thing as perfect parents. Learning and improving are a part of all our lives.

Punishment

☐ Punishment does not teach right from wrong.

☐ Punishment is essentially negative as it involves people in authority (parents) asserting power and control over others (children).

☐ Parenting methods that rely on control over children only result in greater misbehavior because children end up seeking more control over their lives and attempt to make choices out of rebellion.

☐ Punishment rarely includes time taken to explain things to children or to show them what is acceptable.

Punishment for actions without an explanation of why does no good in changing behavior.

☐ Punishment does not work to get rid of misbehavior.

In what ways are you using punishment to raise your children? Check off the boxes that apply to your parenting style and/or to the responses of your children. If any boxes were checked, decide how you can transform your punishment style of parenting to align more with the discipline styles listed above. Remember, punishment does not teach right from wrong; thus, it does not promote positive decision-making.

Note: A discipline versus punishment checklist can be found in appendix E.

Move Forward with Discipline, Leave behind Punishment

To do this, you must take a look at your children's environment and begin to change the factors that are contributing to their behavior. When working to make changes, start by looking in the mirror. Change starts with you.

Begin to implement the foundational skills listed in this chapter. You must be ready to learn and use the basic positive discipline skills introduced above so that your planning skills and reactions to situations are beneficial to developing your child's life skills.

So how do you begin this learning process? You already have. If you do nothing else right now but continue reading the first five chapters of this book, you are well on your way to taking the right steps to improving your knowledge of how to be a successful parent.

Read on.

Communication

Communication is very important. Hearing verbal communication and seeing nonverbal communication is how our children learn to behave, define their boundaries, and understand the world around them.

When telling your children to do something, try beginning your request by saying "I need you to…" It will be most effective if you use a calm voice, speak slowly, and use eye contact.

Give your children choices. This empowers them and gives them a sense of control. Give no more than two to three choices and select the choices that will result in respectful and responsible behavior. For example, "We need to go grocery shopping and clean the house. Would you like to come shopping with me or stay home with dad and help him clean?

Dealing with a Case of the Grumps

Moody children aren't just experienced by parents during the teenage years. Children (and adults) of all ages can be grumpy at times. When your children are unwilling or unable to communicate their feelings or are unclear about how they feel, try these phrases on for size:

- It appears that you feel…
- It seems to me…
- You believe…
- What I hear you saying is…
- Do you mean…

Counselor's Corner

How do you act when you are in bad mood? How do you treat others when you are upset? What helps you to feel better?

The answers to these questions are what your children will likely do as well. Talk with them about what you do and why you do it. Brainstorm what would help them and reiterate that respect for others is non-negotiable.

Be a positive example!

- Correct me if I am wrong, could it be that...
- Is it possible that...
- Let me see if I understand...

For some children, writing, drawing, or using puppets can make it much easier to convey their feelings and thoughts. Offer these as choices. Not only will choices allow your children to feel more empowered, but using these options of indirect communication makes it much less threatening for them to share their feelings and thoughts.

Over the years, I have seen countless kids open up when a puppet asks them a question. Provide them with their own puppet so they feel that it is their puppet responding, not them.

Time for Action

You tell your children that playtime is over, but you continue to tickle them.

> Question: What will your kids hear?
> Answer: Of course, your words will have no meaning. It is your action of tickling them that sends the message that it is still playtime.

You tell your children that there is no talking in the library. Just then, your phone rings and you have a conversation.

> Question: What did your children learn?
> Answer: Talking in the library is okay.

You tell your children that they will have to go to their room if they do not start listening. You make this threat three more times, and now you are frustrated and are yelling at them.

> Question: What did your children hear?
> Answer: "Blah, Blah, Blah, blah, blah." When your actions do not support your words, your kids may hear your actual words, but they mean

nothing. Only when you follow through on doing what you say will your children take you seriously.

You tell your teenage daughter that she can go shopping with you on Saturday for a prom dress. Saturday comes, and you tell her that she will have to wait another day because there is something that you have to do.

Question: What did you teach your daughter?
Answer: Unless it is an emergency situation, your daughter has learned that you are unreliable. She has also learned that it is okay to go back on her word.

We as parents are the examples that our children look toward the most. If our actions are not in sync with our words, we are teaching our children poor lessons in responsibility, respect, and appropriate behaviors.

> Words are powerful.
> Actions are life changing.

Stopping Behaviors

When children repeat behaviors, they do so because they are not receiving a clear message to stop. This is good news when your child chooses to display positive choices. However, when you are trying to extinguish an inappropriate behavior, you need to be able to communicate the importance of stopping ASAP!

Many people don't realize that they are sending inconsistent messages to their children. The following messages do not tell children to stop a behavior:

- "I wish you would..."
- "You should..."

- Offering a reward *after* your child refuses to comply (this is bribery)
- Saying one thing but then allowing the opposite
- Giving warnings, reminders, and repeating your requests
- Ending a request with, "Okay?"

Sending clear messages of what you expect your children to do/how you expect them to behave must be conveyed consistently. Matching your verbal and nonverbal communication is very important in establishing limits for your child.

When clearly communicating with your children, follow these steps to help avoid blaming, scolding, and negative attention (none of those are effective anyway):

1. Use a calm voice. This shows that you are in control of yourself. It also serves as an example to your children of how to handle problems in a calm manner.
2. Speak about your child's behavior. Simply state that your child is a great person; it is the behavior that needs to change.
3. Tell your child simply and specifically what you expect. "I need you to..."
4. Tell your child the consequences associated with following your request along with the consequences for not following through. (See chapter three to learn about the different types of consequences.)
5. Walk away and give your child some time to make a decision.
6. Always deliver the consequence based on what your child chooses to do.
7. Do all of these things consistently.

Follow these steps each and every time, and you will be amazed at the ways in which your children will show positive behavior choices.

Behavior

A Glimpse of Childhood Behaviors

All behavior has purpose. Depending on our needs and wants, we all act in certain ways to get these needs and wants met. Our behavior is a strong way in which we communicate with others. We can use our words to say one thing, and our behavior will either support our statements or work to negate them. Actions truly do speak louder than words.

Children commonly display the following behaviors. Although frustrating at times, their behavior is trying to tell you something. If you take the time to understand what need or want your child has in the moment, you will be able to teach them how to get the outcome they are looking for without using inappropriate behavior.

- *Tantrums* may indicate several things. Your child may be experiencing strong feelings such as frustration, anger, fear, dislike, anxiety, etc. Another possibility is that your child may not want to complete a task and is trying to escape the activity by using a tantrum. Whatever the case may be, do your best to try to uncover the true need or want behind the tantrum so that your child can be supported to the greatest extent possible with coping skills for each situation. See appendix B for a list of coping skills and activities.

  Truly, when all is said and done, the tantrum should not have helped to solve your child's problem. It should be their coping and problem-solving skills that help them achieve their desired outcome. If your child's tantrum is rewarded by getting their needs and wants met, his throwing tantrums will continue into the future. This cycle will go on as long as you allow it. Put a stop to it today! Refer to the chapter on tantrums for the complete discussion.

- *Avoidance* may indicate that your child is uncomfortable in a given situation. Someone or something may be bothering them. Your child's goal here is to escape. With plenty of support and practice of how to manage uncomfortable feelings, avoidance can be effectively addressed.

  It is wise to seek the help of the mental health professional when working through avoidance. They can objectively work with your child and family as strategies are identified and used.

- *Resistance* to an activity or demand may mean that your child is unclear on what they are to do. Simply clarifying and modeling the steps can resolve this situation quickly.

  Resistance could also mean that your child does not like something and has no desire to participate in the task. Many times, children will state their displeasure with things, but not always. Keep this in mind if your child shows resistance. In these cases, be open to discussing what their choices are and what the expectations will be after the current task is complete. Talking things out and putting a plan in place may be just what your child's resistance needs to take a hike!

- *Aggression* is a clear statement of anger. Typically, children show this behavior in order to get others to leave them alone or to escape an undesirable or uncomfortable situation. As long as your child is not hurting anyone, your best bet is to listen to their communication of "leave me alone."

  Once you notice aggression in your child, it is time to start thinking about how to head it off. When you are both calm, talk with your child to create a plan that gives options for anger management (see appendix C) and their need to be alone. Be certain that they know that is okay to feel angry, but it is not okay to hurt others (emotionally or physically) or to become destructive.

Give your child permission to walk away from a situation that is bothering them to calm down. Teach them other strategies for dealing with strong feelings as presented in appendix B and appendix C. Lastly, teach your child that it is okay to respectfully ask for alone time.

- *Obsessions* can be seen with a variety of items. Over the years, I have worked with children who have been obsessed with bow ties, vacuums, power lines, television characters, historical artifacts, and many more random items that seem to consume their attention.

  At any chance given, they want to look at pictures of their interests, draw their own pictures, research these items, or talk about them with others. Sometimes it is very difficult to get these children to focus on anything but their obsession.

  In a nutshell, if your child has obsessions, it is pretty clear that their interest(s) are much more exciting than what you are attempting to offer at that time.

  Use this to your behavior-planning benefit. You already know what motivates your child, so use it as a positive reward incentive.

  More importantly, if you feel that your child's obsessions are dictating their life choices and/or inhibiting a normal development, consult with your child's doctor as there may be an underlying cause.

- *Physical attention* such as hugs, playing with your hair, wrestling, and holding your hand indicate that you are well liked. Your children's actions are showing you that they enjoy your company and want to be around you. They also figure out how to get attention by first showing attention. This is a powerful lesson. When your child gives a hug, they get a hug back. When they wrestle with mom or dad, they get a wrestling partner to spend time with.

On the other hand, your children may be showing this behavior because they want something from you.

For example, my son knows that I liked my hair played with. When younger, he would conveniently offer to play with my hair just as I finished his bedtime routine in hopes that he would get to stay up just a few minutes longer.

Promote the first of these two possibilities of attention seeking by giving much more energy to your children during appropriate attention-seeking moments.

Counselor's Corner

Spending time together is the perfect way to improve the parent-child bond that you share. There are endless activities to choose from:

Play cards	Set-up a treasure hunt	Read a book aloud
Go swimming	Play tag	Play "I Spy"
Do a craft	Go on a bike ride	Build with blocks
Do a puzzle	Dance	Garden together
Play hopscotch	Visit the local playground or park	Go to the Zoo
Build a fort	Bake	Go to the library
Play hide-and-seek	Play dress-up	Paint
Go shopping	Play an online game	Camp in the backyard

Explanations for Childhood Misbehavior

There are always reasons to explain children's behavior. Heck, there are reasons to explain adult behavior too. As we know, everyone displays different types of behavior based on what their needs and wants are at any given time.

In the case of your children, they may show wonderful behavior because they are trying to get you to praise or reward them. Alternately, misbehavior may be used because they are jealous or are trying to get your attention any way they can.

Ask yourself (or better yet your children) the following questions:

- What are they trying to get by acting this way?
- What are they trying to get out of by acting this way?

I guarantee that there is an explanation and/or a payoff for what they are doing.

Common explanations for children's behavior can be categorized into three general areas: Attention, Power, and Avoiding Failure.

1. Attention

Some children try to get attention from others in any way possible. This includes misbehaving. To them, negative attention is better than no attention at all. If this describes your child, try these strategies on for size:

Strategies to the Rescue!

- *Stand closely to your child.*

Use a serious physical presence so that your child knows that you mean business. Do this by standing closely to your child, and try not to engage with them verbally until the misbehavior stops. Verbal redirection tends to fuel the fire, so to say, especially if an argument results.

> Nonverbal communication is much more effective than words could ever be.

Use signals such as pointing to a chair to tell your child to sit, telling them to walk with you with by waving them on, or shaking your head no. Your child will be able to read your body language and know what you are expecting.

If your child has difficulty with understanding nonverbal signals, create flashcards and keep them on a ring for easy access. Put pictures of appropriate behavior on each card and show the needed card to your child while using physical presence.

These interventions will teach your children how to behave without giving them negative attention.

- *Praise.*

Giving praise during times when your children are behaving well reinforces the fact that they can receive the attention that they need from you when showing appropriate behaviors.

Praise can be in the form of saying nice things to let your children know that you have noticed them, giving a high five, leaving a kind note, or giving a treat. Whatever combination you choose, put some time into noticing and praising your child. The results will amaze you!

Make a big deal when success is seen as well as times where positive effort was made—even if your children don't completely succeed. If you point out and give attention to the positive steps taken, your children will respond by striving to demonstrate positive behavior more and more.

Keep in mind that children will test you. They may not be used to receiving frequent praise for a job well done or even for a partial job well done. Let's face it— we are all busy, and praising others usually isn't at the top of the to-do list. However, you will have to make a change to that to-do list if you want your children to stop misbehaving.

All this talk about praise seems simple. Just say a nice few words, right? Yup, pretty much. Just make sure you do it often and give your children specific examples of what has made you proud. This shows them even more that you are paying attention to the details of their lives.

Remember the magic that we spoke about a few pages back? A big piece of magically preventing misbehavior before it starts begins right here with acknowledging your child's positive choices. Want to get a start on this magic? Look at your children right now and hand over a specific praise. If they look at you funny or don't answer, don't worry. They heard you. Give out other praises before the day is over.

- *Plan.*

Use a formal plan to track praises. Sticker charts, tokens, play money, and so on are all effective ways to give your children tangible praises. Begin your praise by telling your children the specific things that you are proud of and then give them their reward (sticker, token, play money, etc.) as a symbol for a job well done. When a predetermined amount has been earned, they can be turned in for privileges or prizes.

> A global plan for all children in the home to participate in will make the results even better!

These plans work especially well when more than one child participates (frequently this other person is a sibling). This is because children tend to rise to the occasion of doing their best possible when they compete with other children. This healthy competition easily becomes a driving force in encouraging each child to meet their goals at every opportunity.

See appendix A for further ideas on behavior planning.

- *Educate.*

Your children's future depends on the time you spend teaching them how to behave, how to be respectful, and how to be responsible. These are foundational skills that they will need as an adult.

If you don't teach your children these important skills, who will? Let me tell you—the media will, the movie industry will, their friends will, magazines will, the Internet will, song lyrics will, and so on. Do you feel comfortable with these influences guiding your children's future? All of you had better have said no to that question!

In a world driven by money, violence, sex, and selfish living, you cannot and should not expose your children to the inappropriate activities listed above. They all contain adult content and have the potential to negatively influence your children.

When your children eventually encounter these things, have an open conversation about right and wrong. Just because it is on television doesn't mean that it is okay. The same goes for the Internet.

In many instances, television shows aren't even real life. Children have a very difficult time understanding the difference between fantasy and reality. It is up to you to educate them.

It is your job to shelter your children from the ills of the world and then to finally set the record straight by educating them on what they are seeing and how that impacts the expectations that have been set for them.

Counselor's Corner

There isn't a day that goes by where we aren't exposed to some type of inappropriate influence. Children need your help to understand what these things mean for them.

(Hint: the expectations won't change. However, having an understanding of the choices they have and how those choices can impact their future is extremely important.)

Being supported in following expectations despite their life exposures will decrease their need for negative attention-seeking behaviors. Just be prepared to keep the lines of communication open to help your children sort out everything that our culture is telling them each and every day.

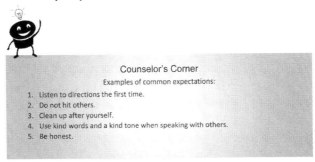

Counselor's Corner

Examples of common expectations:
1. Listen to directions the first time.
2. Do not hit others.
3. Clean up after yourself.
4. Use kind words and a kind tone when speaking with others.
5. Be honest.

• *Do something unexpected.*

This approach is sometimes needed to get your children to stop misbehaving immediately so that they can focus on you. Turn the lights off, clang some pans, turn on some music, talk to an inanimate item such as the wall, change the sound of your voice, and doing a dance are a few ways to refocus your children.

Having a sense of humor and remaining calm will serve you and your children well in these instances. Losing control only shows your children that it is okay to use a negative influence to get what you want, which is the very thing you are trying to teach your children *not* to do.

• *Send your child to a quiet place to think.*

Simply tell your child that they are on a time-out. While in time-out, they are to think about their actions and what they should do differently next time. Do not speak or give any attention to your child while they are in time-out. This is so that your child's negative behavior is not reinforced by giving them exactly what they were looking for to begin with—attention.

If your child attempts to engage you or has a tantrum, calmly say, "We can talk about this when you have sat quietly and thought about what happened." Then walk away. Be prepared to do this more than once and to do so calmly each time.

Your child should be required to sit *quietly* in time-out for one minute per every year of age. If your child is seven, they need to sit in time-out to think for seven minutes. The seven minutes do not start until your child is quiet.

Once complete, your child needs to apologize for any wrongdoings and then talk with you about a plan for improving their behavior in the future. Keep this conversation short and sweet because too much talking can result in your child becoming frustrated and showing misbehavior again. The act of serving the time-out sends a strong message that their behavior was unacceptable all on its own.

Speaking at length is just not necessary. Plus, too much talking about the crime again reinforces your child's misbehavior by giving it a lot of attention. Again, this is what we are trying to avoid!

2. Power

Challenging and argumentative behaviors are commonly seen with children seeking power and control. More severe behaviors such as making threats, breaking things, lying, and manipulating others may also be seen. Children looking for more power and control in their lives want things their way and are not likely to comply with household expectations and caregiver requests. In their minds, compliance equals loss of control. This makes them feel uncomfortable.

Strategies to the Rescue!

- *Maintain a positive relationship.*

    Feeling loved, accepted, and cared for are critical for children. Never tell your children that they are bad; rather, tell them that they made a poor choice when they misbehave.

    We humans learn by making mistakes. Send the message that you will always love your children and will be there to support them in working through life's decisions and mistakes. I tell my kids all the time, "I love you no matter what." As young children, they repeated this back to me frequently. Teaching and showing your children this high level of acceptance and support makes a huge difference in your children's self-esteem.

    When they know that they have your love no matter what, it will foster communication between the two of you. This will greatly benefit your relationship and your children's ability to navigate the world around them. When they communicate with you and they trust you to lovingly answer their many life questions and to have conversations about right versus wrong, trusting relationships between parents and children flourish.

    Don't expect change to happen overnight. Difficult children will not be willing to show positive changes quickly. They will most likely test your sincerity and keep testing to see if your love and support are for real.

It is hard to always take the "high road." I encourage you to stick it out; the payoff will be great.

- *Teach and model social skills.*

  Teaching your children social skills that include the important aspect of empathy for others should be incorporated into everyday interactions. Decide on a skill for the week and practice each day. Each skill should incorporate the treatment of others. Be very careful to always use the skill yourself even if your think your child is not around. Being a positive role model will have the greatest impact. See appendix D for further information on social skill development.

  If you struggle with teaching and practicing social skills with your children, attend family counseling or enroll them in group counseling with other peers. Just as listed above, you must also use the skills that are being/have been taught. To do this, speak with your child's counselor so the skills from counseling can be carried over to daily life.

- *Choose your battles.*

  Whenever possible, avoid direct confrontation by agreeing with your children or changing the subject. Obviously you cannot agree with everything your children say or do, but you can agree to some. Choosing your battles helps to decrease the arguing and allows your children to see that you are listening to them by allowing them what they want when feasible. The following are examples:

  o   You tell your child that they can have one cookie for a snack, but they ask for two cookies. As long as they use their manners to ask for the second cookie, give it to them.

o Your child wants to wear a T-shirt to school in the middle of winter instead of long sleeves. Allow the T-shirt. If they are cold, they will choose more wisely in the future.

o Curfew is 10:00 p.m. but your teenager is asking for 11:30 p.m. Have a conversation and agree on somewhere in between.

The rule to follow here is to make sure your children are safe. Agreeing that your children can do something that is dangerous is not an option. You are the parent, and your primary job is to take care of your children by keeping them safe and meeting their basic needs. There is no wiggle room when it comes to issues of safety.

Each situation listed above does not present danger to your child. Being willing to compromise and to give up some of your control sends a message that you value your child's independence and self-advocacy skills.

When you need to stand your ground and are faced with a confrontation, do your best to remain calm. Talk in a calm voice. State that the decision has been made and once your child can show that they are calm, the conversation can continue.

Tip: Before moving forward with this conversation, make sure that your child's body is *showing* calmness. Children will frequently say that they are calm or ready to talk, but their body language is showing quite the opposite.

> We all want to feel empowered.
> Children are no exception.

- *Recognize the power that your child has and state your next move.*

I have received countless gasps and unbelieving looks from adults as I have made the following statements to children:

○ "You are in control of your own choices."
○ "Adults cannot make you do anything."

I know it seems that by telling children this, I am handing over the world on a silver platter. However, both statements are 100 percent true. It is a fact that we are all in control of the choices we make, kids included. If we are to be honest with ourselves and with our children about being respectful and responsible, then this is the place to start.

Allowing your children to understand that they determine their own destiny creates a sense of healthy empowerment. It also allows children to feel proud of their actions when they succeed. It isn't just children who feel proud when they succeed; it is you and me too. Why not allow your children to take credit for their accomplishments?

Of course, this fact of your children being in charge of themselves doesn't take you off of the parenting hook—not even close! Your children need you to show them the way in life and to hold them accountable for their actions. Without proper guidance, your children will likely make decisions that will negatively impact their success. Yes, they are in control of themselves, but they need you to show them how to use their control. Using the interventions and the positive and negative

When given the opportunity to succeed, children generally rise to the occasion and make the right choice.

consequences listed in this book will help you to do just that.

A great example of recognizing the power that your children have and letting them know what will be coming next can be found below. Use this as your creative launching pad to form your empowering and teaching phrases.

"I can't make you finish your dinner, but we will all be going out for ice cream in ten minutes. If you choose to finish your dinner, you may order some for yourself."

In one teeny, tiny sentence, you have calmly acknowledged your child's power, given choices, and informed them of the consequences linked to their actions—again phrased as their choice. Follow through on your statement. Give the ice cream if it is earned, and withhold it if it is not earned. Doing anything but what you originally stated makes your present and future words meaningless.

- *Do something unexpected.*

If you read the above section on attention-getting behavior strategies, this section will sound strangely familiar. Feel free to read it again.

Doing something unexpected is an approach sometimes needed to get your children to stop misbehaving immediately so that they can focus on you. Turn the lights off, clang some pans, turn on some music, talk to an inanimate item such as the wall, change the sound of your voice, and doing a dance are a few ways to refocus your child.

Having a sense of humor and remaining calm will serve you and your children well in these instances. Losing control only shows your children that it is okay to use a negative influence to get what you want, which is the very thing you are trying to teach your children *not* to do.

• *Always give a choice.*

Who doesn't like to have choices? Adults demand choices. And you know what? We get them. We choose what to eat, what type of car to drive, what to wear, and even whether we stay in bed all day or get up to face the world. Every action we take during the day is based on choices we made. Wow, all of those choices equal a world of responsibility.

Give your children some of the power that they are looking for by providing choices frequently. This should be done even when they are misbehaving. For example, give them two choices of what they can do. Make these choices things that will help to stop the misbehavior and/or solve the problem. A specific example is listed below.

"You may sit quietly and finish eating your dinner or you may go to time-out (or insert another consequence). The choice is yours."

Be prepared to make this statement one additional time. If after those two attempts, your child is still refusing, it is time to send them to time-out or use planned ignoring, and future consequences (loss of privileges). Your decision here will greatly depend on the age of your child.

If your child's behavior results in a time-out, be prepared to have a problem-solving discussion afterwards that will include them finishing their dinner.

Congratulations! You have just learned how to stop misbehavior and work through how to get your child to ultimately make a wise choice. It definitely takes time and patience, but the longer you stick with this approach, the shorter the process will be until it eventually is not needed any longer.

- *Use logical consequences.*

  When your child will not comply and is content with arguing with you every step of the way, it is time to use some of your consequence tools. Refer to the consequences chapter for an in-depth look into types of consequences and how to use each one.

  If you do not already have an established plan of what results in response to your child's misbehavior, look toward logical consequences for help. Examples of how to use logical consequences are listed below.

  Take note that each of these consequences are directly related to the misbehavior. This is why they are called logical consequences.

  ○ If your child refuses to eat dinner = no snacks.
  ○ If your child lies to you about where they were with a friend = they are no longer allowed to hang around with that friend for a certain period of time.
  ○ If your child watches an unapproved television show = they lose television privileges.
  ○ If your child uses their cell phone when they are not allowed to = they have no cell phone to use.

  > Logical consequences make sense.
  > The result is greater learning

  Logical consequences help children learn from their actions in very effective ways because the consequences are directly linked to the misbehavior. Be prepared to follow through on the consequences every time. If you are consistent, your children will begin to see that you mean business.

- *Involve all people who interact with your child, plus more.*

Chances are, your children are not only acting out at home. Keep the lines of communication open with daycare providers, school staff, coaches, and other people who care for your children.

Gain their input on what behaviors they are seeing. Find out what things have helped make the situation better and what things have made the situation worse. Share with them the plans that you have for your home and request that they maintain frequent communication with you.

Counselor's Corner
Reality Check!!
Your children need to learn through your teaching and showing before you can expect compliance. By now, you are well aware that kids test the limits. It is up to you and other caregivers to use these challenging behavioral times as teachable moments. Helping your children to understand why a behavior is or is not acceptable is a huge step in giving them logical reasons to make positive choices.

Many behavior programs can incorporate an away-from-home piece that serves as a report of choices that your child made throughout the day. Positive and negative consequences need to apply to away behavior just as they do for home behaviors.

Meet with your child's caregivers to agree upon a system that is manageable and effective for both of you. Do not demand that they use what you are proposing. Compromise and consideration for others is necessary if you want the plan to succeed. Sample home-to-school behavior plans can be found in appendix A.

Consideration should be given to informing your child's doctor about the behaviors that you are observing. Global care that involves a medical professional being aware of this aspect of your child can help to address all your child's needs. It is doing your child a disservice when this vital piece of information about their development is left out.

Seeking out a mental health professional for individual and family counseling is another professional to involve as well. Mental health professionals are trained in helping individuals and families work through difficult times and can help everyone to identify positive coping skills. Your child's physician or school will be able to make appropriate local referrals—just ask!

3. Avoiding Failure

Some children begin to think that they can't live up to the expectations set by their caregivers or even themselves. In an attempt to deal with these negative thoughts and feelings, they misbehave in ways that make them appear unable to succeed. Examples include procrastinating, not completing their chores, or pretending to not understand tasks by needing constant help.

These children hope that everyone will decide to stop trying and just leave them alone so they won't have to face that they aren't performing up to their potential.

Strategies to the Rescue!

• *Acknowledge and remind.*

For some children, it is enough for a caregiver to simply show empathy over a difficult task. Simply acknowledging that something is difficult for your child shows your support and may provide the encouragement your child needs to ditch their inappropriate behaviors.

Remind your children of past successes they have had. Reflecting upon how they succeeded in related situations can help to give them hope of also being successful in the present moment. If necessary, walk them through step by step of what needs to be done. They will not only feel supported but also proud of their accomplishments!

Acknowledging and reminding helps to promote an attitude of perseverance and thoughts of "I can succeed."

Parents have a tough job. Be dedicated and patient as your children work to improve their "I can" attitude.

- *Build confidence.*

The simplest way to build your children's confidence is to use your words and actions. As an added bonus, use specifics when identifying the wonderful things your child is doing (or has done). Being specific lets your child know exactly what you are proud of and what they should repeat in the future.

"You are using wonderful effort in coloring your picture. I notice how you are using blue and orange very neatly."

"You scored two goals during soccer today. You are really getting good. Your team is lucky to have you."

"I see that you earned a B on your last social studies test. I am proud of you! You made a really good decision to spend all that time studying."

"Thank you for helping your sister with her homework. You have been a great help to her. We are blessed to have such a kind person in our family."

If you are searching for a praise to give, enlist the help of your children. Ask them to show their little sibling how to do something, ask them to show you how to do something, or ask their opinion on how you could have done something better. Be sure to give plenty of praise during and after they complete the task. Even if things don't work out well, praise the effort given and any areas that were a success.

Some parents I know really struggle finding areas to praise. They feel that their child is always doing something to gain attention or power or to avoid failure. Although it sounds silly, they were willing to try building their child's confidence by praising their child for doing things that are normally done each day.

For example, when your child goes to bed, thank them for turning off the light and tell them that you are happy with their consideration for helping to save money on the electric bill. When your child puts their shoes on before leaving the house, thank them for doing their part to keep their socks clean and feet safe. These are examples of things that your child may do automatically; the difference is that you are now recognizing them for these actions as a stepping stone to improving future behaviors.

As I said before, it sounds silly. However, finding areas to positively praise can result in many benefits. For best results, be prepared to use this strategy often. You'll have to be creative to pull this off, but you can do it! I know this because you love your children and are here reading how to be the best parent out there. Kudos!

- *Slow down and take it one step at a time.*

Confidence naturally develops when we feel good about a job well done. However, if we feel overwhelmed by responsibilities, we have a difficult time getting any job done at all. I know that when I have many things to accomplish, it is hard to focus on just one thing at a time. Doing a little of everything creates chaos in my brain and after a few hours of operating like this, I feel discouraged and very overwhelmed that nothing has been fully completed.

Overwhelmed is a good word to describe how children feel when they are given too many instructions at a time or when we expect perfection.

Too many instructions + demanding perfection = low confidence and failure.

In comparison to your life, your children have had a short amount of time to learn how to behave and to perform tasks that you are asking of them.

Consider for a moment that

- you have had many more years to learn from your mistakes;
- you have had many more years to understand what behaviors are expected in various situations; and
- you have had many more years to learn how to do the laundry, the dishes, and other chores that you may be asking your children to do.

Your children need and deserve grace. Grace gives your children leeway along with your understanding and acceptance that everything does not have to be perfect. As long as they are trying their best, it is good enough for you.

GRACE IS A
WONDERFUL THING.

Giving one-step requests helps to lessen anxious feelings about forgetting to do something. It builds confidence as each step is met with success followed by the next.

Which example below do you think your child will have the most success with?

1. "When we get home, I need you to pick out your clothes for school tomorrow. Then you need to feed the dog and get started on your homework. If you need help with your homework, let me know."
2. "Please go upstairs and pick out an outfit to wear to school tomorrow."

(Child completes this task and is told "thank you" and/or "nice job matching your clothes.")

"Please feed the dog. The new bag of dog food is in the garage."

(Child completes this task and is told "thank you" and/or "nice job.")

"Please start your homework. I will check on you soon to see how things are going."

(Child completes this task and is told "thank you" and/or "nice job getting started right away.")

If you picked number 2, you are right. Each step is separated out, which guides and supports your child to get the job done independently and without anxiety.

- *Post positive messages.*

    Show your children that you are proud of them and how much you love them by displaying your feelings for them to see throughout the day.

    This can be done by

    ○ hanging their artwork or schoolwork on the fridge for all to see,
    ○ taping a kind note to the bathroom mirror so they see it in the morning,
    ○ packing a confidence-building note in their lunch,

- ° sending them a text message now and then giving them specific praise,
- ° showing off trophies or awards that they have won, and
- ° talking positively about their actions in front of others.

Even if your children do not outwardly show that they appreciate these gestures, I guarantee you that they are smiling inside from all the positive attention.

Children need and want to know that they are doing a good job. If they don't hear it or see it, expectations begin to become fuzzy, and an increase of testing behaviors may be seen.

- *Teach positive self-talk.*

Changing someone's outlook on life and changing someone's opinion of themselves can begin with using positive self-talk.

Positive self-talk is when we tell ourselves how wonderful we are or that we know we can succeed. With that said, let's draw the line between people who brag about how wonderful they are versus people who give themselves a confidence boost. Your children need the second—a confidence boost.

The best way to identify positive self-talk that will fit your child's individual needs is to decide which statements will be most beneficial for your child. These statements should be easy to remember in order for your child to use them as a daily confidence boost. Consider some of the following:

- ° "I know I can do it."
- ° "I have been through this before and I was fine. I know I can do it again."

- ○ "I am really good at math. I will get a good grade on this test."
- ○ "If I need help I can ask _____. Everything will be okay."
- ○ "I am strong and courageous."
- ○ "Take it one step at a time."
- ○ "In with the good thoughts and out with the bad."

Talk with your child about what phrases will be the most beneficial. Have them try one or two for a few days and make note about times when they used a phrase and what the results were. Recording this information will help to further identify their needs and what strategies are most helpful.

Reflect on your children's progress daily and encourage the continued use of positive self-talk. Be willing to make changes if needed.

Lastly, it can be helpful for your children to hear that everyone, even adults, need to use positive self-talk. It is a healthy coping skill to use throughout life.

Intervention

This may sound strange, but it is true: the best time to intervene in your child's misbehavior is when the misbehavior is *not* happening.

Nope, that wasn't a typo. It is a fact—address your children's misbehavior when they are making positive choices. Let me tell you why.

Some children think (and are usually right) that they get a bigger response from adults when they use negative behavior. This is because when they are making positive choices, their parents and caregivers don't always acknowledge them.

Let's be honest: when our children are following the rules, we tend to take it for granted and don't expend the extra energy on letting them know that we noticed their positive choices. In fact, some of us have the thought that our children *should* act "good" all the time automatically. No recognition needed.

However, when they make poor choices, do we notice? You better believe we do! Not only do we notice, but we also yell, we give consequences, and we make a big to-do. All of that for what? Unfortunately, the answer to this question creates a gigantic mess in the world of behavior management.

The Answer

A huge amount of attention is given to your children when they misbehave. In other words, when children misbehave, they are always being acknowledged. Uh-oh!

Do you see the problem here? When we consider the amount of time given to inappropriate behavior versus appropriate behavior, it begins to make sense why children continue their poor behavior choices—because it meets several of their needs. These needs include such things as attention, power, control, and avoidance.

In the minds of these children, they want their parents' acknowledgement, and they have learned that the only way they can get it is to misbehave.

The fantastic news in all of this is that you have the power to make it all change. Hooray!

Begin changing this learned behavior with your children by doing the following things (all of which occur while your children's misbehavior is *not*):

- Tell your children what you observed them doing that made you proud. No matter how small the deed, make sure your children know that you noticed by giving plenty of praise. When you do this, you are increasing the likelihood of these preferred behaviors happening more often.

- Give praise regularly throughout the day when rules are not being broken. Do *not* assume that your children know that you are happy with their actions. "I like how you are sitting patiently for me. You are doing a wonderful job in showing me how mature you are" or "Thank you for eating your dinner without being asked" are some examples.

- Always stay calm when your children break a rule. Give a consequence calmly without a long speech. "You said a swear word so now you have to go to time-out" is enough to get your message through. Giving your time and energy to the negative act of the broken rule only strengthens your children's beliefs that they can get more attention from you for breaking the rules.

- When praising your children, keep it positive, clear, and specific. This type of praise helps your children's self-esteem increase because they begin to see that you take the time to notice them when they are behaving well.

- Use plenty of positive expression and emotion in your acknowledgements. Smile, use an enthusiastic voice, give a high five, do a dance, and whatever else that will convey your message of feeling happy and proud of your children.

Take the time to...

- enjoy every moment with your children,
- sit back and take note of all the wonderful characteristics that your children have,

- be thankful for the happy days and the cuddles that youngsters give,
- be grateful for the times that your children offer to help with the chores,
- relish in the moments when your children confide in you,
- enjoy laughter and time spent together,
- celebrate accomplishments and milestones together, and
- feel proud as you reflect on your children's life in amazement of how they have grown and all they have learned.

It is up to you to mold your children. My, how blessed you are to have such a privilege in life.

Hang in there. Be tough. Never give up.

Consequences

Consequences are a delicate matter. Many people think of consequences as punishment. This thinking is only half-right. Consequences occur as a result of actions and are most effective when given *immediately* and *consistently* after a behavior occurs.

It is okay to give your children one warning or reminder. Any more than that is too much.

More than one warning sends the message that your children really don't have to listen the first, second, or even third time. By this time, you are losing your cool and your children are still defying you.

Counselor's Corner

Appropriate behavior will NOT increase if the inappropriate behavior continues to be reinforced.

When the need or want driving the behavior is being met, that behavior will continue.

This defiance isn't necessarily being done on purpose. Rather, your children are more likely to have gotten used to receiving several warnings. Their choice to not respond right away is what we call learned behavior.

What You Need to Know about Reinforcing Positive Behavior

Learned behavior is serving a need or a want for your children. This need/want is likely being reinforced by your behavioral reactions. For example, if your children frustrate you to the point of yelling at them, they have met their need for your attention. If you go to the store without them because they refused to get ready, they may have met their desire to stay home. Each child has a unique set of reinforcers that they crave in order to meet their need and wants. These reinforcers have a direct relationship on whether behaviors will increase or decrease.

The way in which behavior is reinforced is determined by the reinforcer used, not the intent of the person giving it.

In other words, if your intent is to reduce your children's misbehavior by lecturing and hovering to monitor their behavior, you will find that their misbehavior and defiance will likely increase. Why? You thought you were doing the right thing by showing your children how much you love them by staying close and sharing your thoughts. However, we already know that lectures and a lack of healthy independence do not have a positive impact on our children's behavior. Despite your intentions being good, the end result will not be positive.

The good news is that you can begin now by using your newly found parenting knowledge to reinforce desirable behavior and to decrease your children's misbehavior.

The Secret Ingredient

The secret to using consequences is teaching your children that they are in charge of themselves. Help them understand that the choices they make are connected to natural and logical consequences. It is not you as the parent who makes consequences a reality; it is solely their actions that dictate what consequences will be experienced. Ultimately, your goal is to help your children see the connection between making positive choices to get what they need and want.

When your children are able to admit that they have made poor choices and state that they need to make changes, they have taken a humongous step in the right direction. When this happens, you should feel incredibly proud of your children. If they have not yet come to this realization, it is okay. Continue to support them in recognizing that they are in control of their choices and of the resulting consequences.

Regardless of your children's level of understanding of this concept, the best thing you can do is to remind them of their choices and show them how their actions and consequences are related at every opportunity.

Keep on Truckin'

Perseverance is the name of the game. Keep teaching your children right from wrong by using your newfound knowledge thus far. Have them identify how their behavior affects themselves and others around them. This helps them to reflect on what should stay the same and what things need to change. Additionally, this exercise helps to develop their empathy for others.

Continue to point out the link between *their* behavior and received consequences.

When speaking with your children about their behavior and future goals, use these questions to help guide the conversation:

1. What problem(s) do you think need fixing?
2. What are some things you can do to help fix these things?
3. What are some things I can do to help?
4. How can we prevent these problems from happening in the future?

The Nitty-Gritty on Consequences

It is best to have a clear beginning and a clear ending to every consequence. For example, if the consequence is a time-out, your children need to be told when it is starting and when it will end (by the way, time-out does not start until your child is sitting quietly and still). If the consequence is loss of screen time, your children need to be told beginning and ending times/days. Do not keep these details a mystery.

Nitty-Gritty Types of Consequences

The following are three important types of consequences:

1. Natural
2. Positive
3. Negative

Each of these consequences work together to create positive learning experiences for your children.

If I stay up late, I am tired the next day. If I am a kind person, more people will like me. These are examples of *natural* consequences.

If I work really hard, my consequence is earning a raise. If your child turns in their homework every day for a month, they earn an award. These are examples of *positive* consequences that result from a positive action.

If I am late to work many times, my consequence is getting fired. If I drive too fast, my consequence is getting a speeding ticket. These are examples of *negative* consequences that result from a negative action.

We all earn natural, positive, and negative consequences each day. For us adults, these are generally handed to us in the form of natural consequences (things that happen naturally as a direct result of our actions, such as getting a cavity because we didn't floss or by an authority figure such as our boss (could be positive or negative).

Children have a lot of potential people in their life giving them consequences throughout each day. Parents, teachers, day-care providers, a friend's parent, relatives, and neighbors are some people who may come in contact with your children frequently.

I know that hearing that your children receive consequences throughout the day sounds scary for those of you who are still conditioned to think that consequences equal punishment. The reality is that natural, positive, and negative consequences work together to teach your children right from wrong. This is a good thing.

For children who strive to make positive choices each day, they are exposed to many positive consequences. This is wonderful news for them and for you. These are the children who have a secure self-esteem and who are confident in their choices. In all likelihood, their parents are using the parenting strategies described in this book.

Children of these families typically do not need to resort to misbehavior in an attempt to get their needs and wants met. Positive consequences such as verbal praise, privileges, freedoms, treats, prizes, and so on come frequently enough that they have a clear understanding and motivation to make positive choices. What a fantastic place to be!

Bringing It All Together
into One Neat Little Package

Now that we have taken a glimpse into natural, positive, and negative consequences, let's put them together to create the best benefit for your family.

Natural consequences are automatically part of positive and effective discipline. They occur without your intervention. For example, if your children do not eat breakfast, they will be hungry before lunch. If they refuse to wear a heavy coat when it is cold outside, they will be cold. If children run in flip-flops, they might fall and get hurt. These are considered natural consequences because the consequence happens on its own without your intervention.

> **Counselor's Corner**
> Natural vs. Logical Consequences
>
> Natural consequences can quickly turn to logical consequences.
> If your child is running toward the road are you going to allow a natural consequence to teach the lesson of safety? Of course not! You will grab your child and provide a logical consequence to teach them to stay away from the road.
> Taking away the privilege of outside time for the remainder of the day would be an example of an appropriate and logical consequence.
>
> When it comes to safety, your job as parent is to intervene. Natural consequences have no place in situations like these.

This form of consequence is truly the most effective way of teaching an individual because it happens automatically. You, however, are there to be the hero who reflects on the situation with your child to give plenty of praise or to plan for a different outcome in the future. This is an example of a perfect system.

But what do you do when it is not perfect? Is that even possible when using natural consequences? It all seems to make sense and flow easily. However, we know that learning doesn't only consist of natural consequences. You will need to use logial positive and negative consequences as the basis to your family's behavior plans and as a compliment to the natural consequences that occur.

Positive consequences result from your children obeying your requests, rules, and expectations.

Creating and using positive consequences are fun for everyone. You and your children should sit down to identify their interests and what they would like to work toward. Including them in this process gives them motivation to do well since earning the chosen rewards will contain many of their ideas.

Your children may ask for tangible things like toys or other items; these are fine things to work toward. However, if you choose to have other options available, I encourage you to think outside the box and offer things like an extra snack, a sleepover with a friend, extra television or video game time, no chores for two days, and so on. Further ideas can be found in appendix A.

Write the agreed upon rewards down in a behavior plan that includes what expectations need to be met. You can use a charting system, a journaling system, or whatever works best for your children. They need to be able to refer back to what they are working toward and what they need to do in order to earn their positive consequences.

Counselor's Corner

No one likes to be told what to do or how things are going to be. The truth is that we have to deal with it sometimes, but we don't have to like it.

The same is true for your children. If you hand a plan to them and say that they have to follow the expectations and then show them what they will get in return it may spark a little interest but it won't last.

Creating the expectations and positive consequences together provides for feelings of control, power, and excitement over their own plan. They will be more likely to follow through on what you are asking and to stick with it.

Counselor's Corner
Is it Bribery?

Offering children something in return for their appropriate behavior is seen by some as an incredible resource tool for helping to mold children's behavior. On the other hand, some believe that this method is just plain bribery.

Without a doubt there is some grey area that exists – to the untrained eye that is.

Bribery exists after a child will not comply and the adult in charge resorts to offering a desired item or privilege if only the child will do what they are being asked. This teaches children that they can get what they want by initially not complying...chances are that this isn't the first time that this lesson of non-compliance has been taught.

Using rewards as a motivator and a teaching tool comes when a pre-established plan is agreed upon between the parent and child *prior* to the request. The child knows what positive consequences are able to be earned based on their performance. This, ladies and gentleman, is NOT bribery. This is learning.

Think about your own life....

Why do you go to work? Most of you would say for the paycheck.

Why do you do the laundry? To have clean clothes.

Why do you pay the bills? So you can keep your utilities on.

See that, you make choices to receive rewards every day and you probably never even thought of it that way.

When a child is consistently acknowledged for making positive choices, the drive to receive items or privileges slowly begins to change to desiring to do the right thing solely because they know deep down that it is in fact the right thing to do.

Negative consequences occur in response to your children misbehaving, but I'm sure you have already guessed that. Just as was the case with positive consequences, you need to have these pre-established within your children's plan prior to using them when possible. Make the negative consequence fit the misbehavior. In other words, use a consequence that is related to the behavior that you are trying to change.

For example, if your child knows that they will serve a time-out and write an apology letter for pushing a sibling, they will be less likely to push given that they know what the consequences will be. This will be true *only* if you follow through on the consequences every time the pushing occurs. As an added bonus, serving a time-out allows your child to be removed from the situation in order to make a plan for better behavior choices in the future.

Never, ever give a negative consequence that includes you hitting or name-calling. These behaviors serve as an unintended teaching tool. Unfortunately, this teaching is the opposite of what we are going for here. If you use hitting, yelling, or name-calling to solve the problem of misbehavior, your children will likely follow your example to hit, yell, and call others names to solve their problems. Your children learn that these are acceptable behaviors because they are following your example.

This is bad news all around.

Counselor's Corner

The approach we use is the approach we teach.

The way in which we approach consequences is teaching our children a lesson about acceptable behavior. If we use hurtful means in applying a consequence, we teach hurtful problem-solving. If we use patience, a calm voice, and understanding we teach those positive ways to interact with one other.

I know this makes sense on paper, but what really happens when parents are in the moment and feeling overwhelmed? Like you, I have been there many times. Things don't always go as planned even when you try to do things right.

Picture this: The children start to argue. They are not sharing. Now they are hitting.

Of course this all takes place in a matter of seconds before you can truly intervene. The knee jerk reaction is to yell. For some of you, you may try to hit your children to try to show them how it feels to be hit in an attempt to teach them not to hit others. Yelling and hitting may be helpful to get your children to stop in the moment, but what about the long-term?

In the brains of young children, they think, "Mommy just yelled at us and hit one of us. That must be how people solve their problems."

Clearly this is not what you intended to teach your children, but you did. In fact, this is probably why your children resorting to hitting one another!

I am glad you are open to learning a different approach. Welcome!

How to Correct Misbehavior

1. Ensure that your child understands how to act appropriately. If they do not, take the time right now to teach them by telling, showing, and practicing. Using your words,

modeling the skills, and practicing with your child will ensure complete understanding.

2. If your child chooses to misbehave, calmly give *one* warning/reminder of the desired behavior.

3. If your child chooses to continue the misbehavior, calmly provide a preestablished or logical consequence.

4. Once the consequence is served, make a plan with your child about improved behavior for the future.

5. Tell your child that you love them no matter what.

How to Deliver Consequences Effectively

You now know that all types of consequences need to be directly related to your children's actions in order to have the greatest impact on improving behavior. To ensure that consequences will be a good match to promote desirable behavior, use this checklist. Also, see appendix F for this handy tool.

☐ The consequence is directly linked to my child's behavior.

☐ The consequence is given immediately or as soon as possible after the behavior.

☐ The consequence is given each time the behavior is used.

☐ The consequence is developmentally appropriate for my child.

☐ The consequence is not too severe or too mild to convey understanding.

☐ The consequence is used to positively teach my child about appropriate behavior.

☐ Negative and logical consequences are given with as much privacy as possible.

☐ The consequence is given in an environment that has little to no distractions when possible.

☐ Negative and logical consequences are given in a respectful manner, void of put downs, yelling, hitting, and name-calling.

- Negative and logical consequences are given in a calm manner.
- Brief discussion takes place regarding how consequences and appropriate behaviors apply to current childhood issues as well as how they will apply when my child is an adult.
- My child knew of the positive or negative consequence prior to it being given.
- My child is able to tell me what they did to earn the consequence given.
- When a negative or logical consequence is given, my child can tell me the choices available for improving future behavior.

What Consequences Could Be Making My Child's Behavior Worse?

The answer may surprise you. Thousands of parents give numerous reactions each and every day to their children's behaviors. If you take the time to dissect what is going on, you may find that your responses are giving your children's misbehavior more power rather than deterring it from happening.

Ask yourself, "What occurs after my child's misbehavior that may be causing it to happen in the first place?" Perhaps it is that your children get your attention. Maybe they get out of a responsibility. Whatever the case, think about what consequences (natural, positive, negative, and/or logical) are occurring in direct relation to your children's behavior to see if those consequences are giving your children an incentive to continue the misbehavior into the future.

If you are successful in identifying what may be maintaining your children's misbehavior, you can then start to make plans for how this can change. You can control only one person—yourself! Make a plan to change your reactions and to create suitable consequences.

For more help identifying what could be strengthening your child's misbehavior and for positive ideas to help manage it; visit the Member's Corner at behaviorcorner.com

Wrapping Up

Knowing ahead of time what will naturally happen, what great things will happen, and what undesirable things will happen gives your children a good sense of their boundaries and what to expect from daily life.

When using a negative consequence, you and your children should plan to start over again with a clean slate after the consequence is served. Be ready to move on and be done with the misbehavior after the consequence is done. We all make mistakes, and everyone deserves a fresh start!

Consequences are like barriers; they need to be in place in order to stop and prevent undesirable behaviors. They serve to hold children accountable for their positive and negative actions. Consequences give clear answers to your children's testing behaviors as kids naturally investigate what is acceptable and what is not.

Testing to see if the consequences are here to stay or if they will occur each time is common, especially in the beginning of a new plan. You must be consistent in order to gain the most positive results for your family, yourself included. This consistency will help to decrease the amount your children will test, and before you know it, testing the limits will begin to occur less frequently.

If you are consistent (you have to be; sorry, there is no choice here), your children will learn that you mean what you say. They will feel secure to take healthy risks in life. They will also develop levels of respect and responsibility that you will both be proud of.

This process should be in place for all of the years spent raising your children. If you haven't started yet, start now. It is never too late to devote time to teaching your children right from wrong.

Of special note: Children who act out for the purpose of receiving attention will test the limits and the consequences even more so than others. This is due to their overwhelming need to gain attention. In their minds, negative attention is better than no attention at all. If they can ruffle your feathers and get further consequences, their testing behavior has just paid off (in the form of your attention being given to them), and they will be likely to do it again in the future. The same holds true for when lectures or warnings are given.

Stay calm, consistent and carry on; you will see this behavior decrease.

Reminder: The main goal is to teach, not to punish.

Counselor's Corner

My soap box on those negative attention seekers...

You have already read about children who are content in obtaining any type of attention, even negative. They suck our energy by always testing the limits set for them, seemingly to always be in trouble, and taking advantage of our gracious warnings and reminders.

Well, here is your wake-up call. You can make all of that stop - yes you!

Make changes in your children's environment and these annoying attention seeking behaviors will be on the decline for sure.

Unfortunately, children receive more of our attention when a rule is broken than for behaving well. We tend to take their compliance for granted as we smile and think to ourselves that it is good that our children are acting well. On the other hand, if they don't behave we let them know about it. Now we have created no reason for our children to act responsibly. They get very little of our energy or acknowledgement for doing so. If you were them, why would you choose to follow the rules? Where is the payoff in that?

Answer:

There isn't one. Their only way they receive your attention is by breaking the rules. Time to change that!

Solution:

Give your child plenty of attention for following your rules and expectations (hugs, thumbs up, a special treat, a sticker...). When you have to issue a negative consequence, do it without emotion and do it every time a rule is broken. Do not allow your child to engage with you or to alter your decision. Walk away and end the conversation.

Think of yourself as a gardener who is caring for a garden (your child) by providing plenty of water and sunshine (positive recognition). When weeds (misbehavior) grow, they need to be eliminated. If weeds are allowed to grow, they over-take the beautiful flowers (positive behavior). Don't care for the weeds (misbehavior) by giving them positive recognition.

Once a consequence is served and the behavior is reflected upon through future planning, your child needs to get right back to finding success and using positive behaviors to win your attention.

Ahhh....happiness and harmony!

How to Use the Interventions

The interventions that await you can be used with children and adolescents of all ages. Although numbered, they are not placed in any particular order of importance. It is your job to consider your child's age, abilities, and situation when choosing which intervention(s) to use.

All the interventions are listed by specific behaviors, and many focus on diagnosable mental disorders. The most common behavior concerns along with the most common mental disorders that may occur during children's developmental period (from birth to eighteen years) are included. In addition, mental disorders are listed with an asterisks on the contents page for easy reference. Since the criteria that define these disorders can sometimes be tricky to understand, the defining characteristics are laid out in an easy-to-read format using everyday language. To further simplify this information, each behavior and disorder is categorized by the following three reference points:

- *Introduction* to the behavior or mental disorder
- *Formal diagnosis* as defined by the American Psychiatric Association
- *Interventions* that put you on the path to improving behaviors

These three categories that are listed in each chapter are also broken down by page number in the contents page. Now you don't have to hunt for what you need. Isn't it nice to have something in life that is easy?

Given all of this, I am confident that you will find exactly what you are looking for to improve your child's behavior and wellness.

Combined with the support of this book, online support at behaviorcorner.com, and close work with your child's pediatrician and with a mental health professional, you will find endless interventions for common childhood behaviors that parents like you are struggling to resolve.

You will find easy-to-use strategies within each behavior section. You may even find additional interventions listed in related chapters. For example, if you are interested in finding help to improve your child's listening skills, you will find ideas in the "Does Not Listen" section as well as finding other ideas to spark your thinking in the "Attention, Impulsivity, and Hyperactivity" and "Tantrums" chapters.

The purpose of listing several intervention possibilities is to give you a solid bank of choices. Start by taking some time to consider how a few of the choices would fit your child's personality and needs. Make adjustments and changes as necessary. You can always refer back to the master list when looking to revamp things.

No two children are alike. No two children have the exact same needs or interests. Be willing to try new things, and not just the things that worked for your other kids or for your neighbor's kids. You know your children best; cater to their unique needs.

This process requires patience. Who am I kidding? Parenting in general requires patience. Expect that you and your children will be working closely together to refine and use interventions. Allowing for your child's input will give them a lot of power to succeed.

Tweak as you go. I have never seen a plan or intervention be implemented and be carried out just as it started. Children require newness. They require compromise. They require understanding. All of these things need to be considered as changes are made to the interventions being used.

All of this may or may not mean that a completely different strategy is selected from the list of ideas. It could just simply mean that your child needs a slightly different approach, incentive, or motivator in order to continue their success. Whatever the case, be willing to show how much you love your children, how proud you are of them, and that you value their opinion by compromising with them.

In this fast-paced world, it is hard to consider adding one more thing to the to-do list. Creating and implementing interventions to improve your children's behavior requires dedication. I assure you, that dedication is well worth it.

Think about it; will it be the time you spend watching television that will have a positive impact on your children's functioning, or will spending the time to make personal changes to help mold their present and future be most beneficial? It is a no-brainer if you ask me! Choose wisely.

Adjustment Disorder

Introduction

Despite life's many ups and downs, I bet we could all name a few wonderful times that can make us smile now and into future years.

On the flip side, we have had times that we wish we could forget. Children are no different. They can easily speak about happy times and also about times that made them sad, angry, and upset.

> All children react to life changes and stressors in their own way and in their own time.
> Their level of coping may quickly change. Be there for them every step of the way!

We all deal with life events and feelings in different ways. If your child is one who can express their feelings and needs in healthy ways and move forward by showing resiliency, it will serve them well in life.

For others, stress can become overwhelming, and adjusting to certain stressful situations may be seen as unobtainable.

We all need help sometimes, and that is okay!

Common childhood stressors may include the following:

- the separation or divorce of their parents

- violence in the home

- a move to a new home or a new school

- the birth of a new sibling

- the death of a family member or pet

- change in parent's routine or work schedule

Counselor's Corner

Regardless of how your child reacts to changes and stress, the best thing you can do is to offer your complete support.
- Talk to them without distractions
- Answer their questions the best way you can while considering how much information to share based on their developmental age
- Check-in with your child frequently to see how they are doing and if they need anything

- a parent becoming incarcerated
- foster care placement
- A new step-parent or their parent's significant other living in the home
- Other – each child is different and will react to situations in their own way

In the majority of stressful situations, children (and adults) manage to cope and move forward with little to no negative effects. However, if struggles are still being experienced after a few months, your child may be suffering from an adjustment disorder.

Formal Diagnosis

According to the American Psychiatric Association, adjustment disorder is defined by the following:

- The presence of emotional or behavioral symptoms that result from an identifiable stressor (or stressors).

    The emotional or behavioral symptoms must appear within three months of when the stressor(s) began in the person's life and must present with one or both of the following:

- The response (symptoms) given to the stressor(s) must be in excess of what would normally be expected. When making this determination, consideration must be given to the situation and to the person's culture.
- The response (symptoms) significantly impairs the person daily functioning.

Common Co-Existing Conditions

- Depression
- Attention-deficit/hyperactivity disorder
- Posttraumatic stress disorder
- Substance use
- Suicide risk
- Conduct disorder
- Other mental disorders
- Medical disorders

Adjustment disorder will not be the primary diagnosis if the symptoms are better explained by another mental disorder.

However, adjustment disorder is commonly diagnosed along with other mental disorders if deemed appropriate to the situation.

More and more cases of adjustment disorder in children are being diagnosed. In my experience, I have seen that there are several parenting factors that may unfortunately contribute to the likelihood of an adjustment disorder being diagnosed:

- inconsistent parenting styles
- frequent changes in caregivers
- parents who put their own needs before their child's
- lack of support for their children during times of life stress or change

> Living unselfishly for your children makes huge positive differences in their lives!

These are just few possible issues that could trigger or worsen an emotional or behavioral response.

Now that you know what *not* to do, let's take a look at symptoms of adjustment disorder and then explore what you can do to help.

Possible symptoms include the following:

- defiance may increase
- anger
- arguing or fighting with others may be seen for the first time or be on the rise
- breaking the rules at home, at school, and/or in the community
- making reckless decisions
- drug use
- crying
- change in sleep patterns
- change in appetite
- anxiety
- feeling overwhelmed
- physical symptoms such as headaches, stomachaches, rapid heartbeat

- difficulty keeping up with school work
- lack of desire to maintain responsibilities in and out of the home
- thoughts of suicide

As with any disorder or behavioral concern, you as the parent have a lot of power in changing your child's environment. You can also make changes in how you interact and discipline your child based on their needs.

Interventions

1. Be your child's greatest support. Overcoming adjustment disorder can be a reality for your child with the right amount of support, understanding, and love. Friends and family should all be on board with this too. However, you can only control yourself, so step up to be a supportive example. Don't allow your child to be around those who may cause more stress.

2. Find your child a mental health counselor. Early and regular treatment can reduce the amount, intensity, and length of adjustment disorder symptoms. Mental health counseling can also provide you and your child with life skills such as coping skills, decision-making skills, communication skills, impulse control, and the development of a support network. These are wonderful things to have even when adjustment disorder is no longer an issue.

3. Inquire about attending family therapy sessions with your child. Family therapy can promote healthier interactions between everyone in your home. It can also educate family members about adjustment disorder and what effective home-based interventions can work for your family.

4. Ask the mental health counselor about a support group for your child. This intervention's success will greatly depend on your child's age, functioning, and current situa-

tion. Discussing this option with your child and with their providers will help you to decide whether this intervention would be helpful.

5. Visit behaviorcorner.com to arrange online counseling for you and your child.

6. Make an appointment for your child to see their medical doctor. The doctor will gather information about your concerns, and they may recommend a few medical tests to rule out any possible physical problems. They will also assess for other possible mental health concerns. If you haven't already found a mental health counselor, ask your child's doctor for a referral. Medical doctors and therapists can work together to prevent further mental health concerns such as depression. It is very important to keep your child's doctor updated on your child's functioning and treatment being received from other professionals.

7. Empower your child to make independent choices by asking them their opinion when making family decisions.

8. Teach and practice coping skills. Visit appendix B for a list of coping skills. Present a few to your child, practice with them, and decide which ones will be the best fit for your child and for given situations.

9. Make a plan with your child of how to deal with stressor(s) when they arise. Use visual pictures along with words to create the plan. Once the plan is tried, reflect back and record how it worked so that changes can be made where necessary.

10. Praise and reward your child when they use their coping plan to deal with stress. Praise their independence and follow-through. Let them know how proud you are of them.

11. Reassure your child that they are not alone. Other children suffer from stressors as do adults. Finding a support group, talking to those who have dealt with similar stress-

ors, or meeting others who are working through adjustment disorder can be a comfort to your child.

12. Encourage your child to express their feelings, especially when he or she is feeling stressed. If they will not or are not able to talk about their feelings, it is okay. Talking about one's feelings can be hard to do; don't take it personally. Depending on the age and abilities of your child, give some of these a try to encourage expression:

- Use puppets to communicate with your child. Children feel less vulnerable when speaking to a puppet. This is especially true when they themselves are speaking through their own puppet.
- Create a feelings box with your child. Use a shoe box and decorate it together. They can then begin writing down their feelings or drawing pictures to get their feelings and thoughts out. Once complete, they can place their work in the feelings box for safekeeping. Arrange for a daily time for the two of you to look at their feelings together. If that makes your child uncomfortable, they do not have to be there when you look through their feelings box.
- Go to the store together so they can pick out a journal. Journaling helps to express one's thoughts and emotions. It is also a great way to reflect on where one has been and how things are progressing now.

13. Provide your child with daily opportunities for plenty of exercise. Exercise is a large part of physical and mental health. Daily exercise also helps the brain to cope with life's challenges.

14. Encourage your child to engage in preferred activities. It is common for children suffering from adjustment disorder to resist this, but your encouragement might be just the thing they need to begin having fun.

15. Give your child healthy meals to eat and offer healthy snacks. A balanced diet is good for their growth, development, and overall health.

16. Communicate your child's needs to their teacher(s) at school. Making them aware of your child's struggles and creating a plan will help make your child feel more comfortable. This comfort will likely result in greater success in school.

17. Be optimistic. Adjustment disorder does not typically last for long. When provided with support and treatment, your child will be able to beat this disorder.

18. Visit behaviorcorner.com for more information and contact options for getting additional guidance from a professional therapist.

Anger

Introduction

Anger is a natural human emotion. It is up to parents and caregivers to teach children how to manage this strong feeling. Several theories exist to explain why a child may demonstrate anger. All are feasible options.

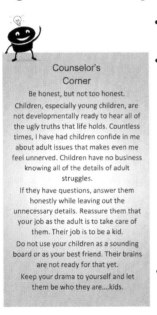

Counselor's Corner

Be honest, but not too honest. Children, especially young children, are not developmentally ready to hear all of the ugly truths that life holds. Countless times, I have had children confide in me about adult issues that makes even me feel unnerved. Children have no business knowing all of the details of adult struggles.

If they have questions, answer them honestly while leaving out the unnecessary details. Reassure them that your job as the adult is to take care of them. Their job is to be a kid.

Do not use your children as a sounding board or as your best friend. Their brains are not ready for that yet.

Keep your drama to yourself and let them be who they are....kids.

- Some families are troubled by great stress that transfers to the children
- Some families overindulge their child, and this creates a child who always wants (and demands) more. When these children don't get their way, anger and tantrums are used in an effort to change their caregiver's mind. Unfortunately, these parents typically give in. This only teaches children that using anger is a viable way of getting what they want in this world.
- Some families use hitting and yelling. This teaches children that they can get what they want by using aggression.
- Some children are violent because they don't see any other way to handle their feelings and are unable to look ahead to see the consequences of their actions. More and more young people today are dealing with adult problems. Their minds and bodies are not ready to process these stresses and the choices that go along with these situations.

- Some families treat children in an abusive or neglectful way. This results in children having unmet developmental needs. They may also have difficulty with showing empathy, making wise decisions, using appropriate social skills, and controlling their impulses.

The common thread in each of these scenarios is that children expect positive outcomes from their aggressive behavior. In fact, they have learned that it works most of the time with their caregivers.

Research has shown that males and females act differently when they are angry. Males typically display anger by acting out, while females tend to internalize anger by becoming anxious, depressed, and withdrawn. Both boys and girls who struggle with anger are likely to have low self-esteem, poor impulse control, and difficulty in judging the intent of others. They also tend to blame others for conflicts with their peers, lack problem-solving skills, and have a hard time accepting responsibility for their actions.

Children undoubtedly need help to learn how to express anger in acceptable ways. When they get angry, they are likely to display inappropriate behavior until taught alternate strategies.

Formal Diagnosis

There is no formal diagnosis for anger alone. Although diagnoses exist with anger as a symptom, no diagnosis addresses anger as the sole symptom.

Interventions

1. Enroll your child as a participant in an anger management or social skills group along with individual and family therapy. Angry children normally have not developed empathy or adequate coping strategies for dealing with anger

and usually have difficulty considering another's perspective. Mental health services can help with these concerns.

2. Visit behaviorcorner.com to arrange for online counseling for you and your child.

3. Communicate your child's needs and anger concerns to their doctor. Allowing your doctor to have this information can be a great help to overall health and wellness treatment.

4. Ensure the presence of strong, consistent, and positive female and male role models in your child's life. Choose people who are tied to your family and who have a desire to be part of your child's life. Bringing in a new adult friend is too risky as their tie to the family is not necessarily a lasting one.

5. Give out nonverbal recognition to your child when you observe positive behavior. This can include a sticker, a smile face on a piece of paper, written words of encouragement, a hug, a thumbs-up, or whatever else you can think of. When your child asks why, you can tell them the specific reason, just smile at them, or say it is because you love them. Any of these three responses will have a positive impact on your child.

6. Reinforce that anger is a natural emotion. However, you must focus directly on the inappropriate behaviors by telling your child that it is not okay to hurt himself, others, or things. Practice the positive choices to deal with anger found in appendix C. If your child is unwilling to engage in this conversation and practice with you, find a mental health therapist or community support system that they can participate in. Fostering this learning must be done now. Learning new ways of coping becomes harder as your child gets older.

7. Talk with your child to estimate the number of times per day that anger outbursts may occur. Provide that exact

number of tangible items (on a checklist or through chips, scraps of paper or fabric, beads, cereal pieces, candy, etc.). For example, if your child displays anger approximately five times per day, set aside five tangible items.

One item must be turned in each time your child displays anger. Make a note of the number remaining at the end of the day in order to show progress. Extra items may be turned in for a reward or can be eaten (edible token items). The number of items provided to your child can begin to decrease after a few consecutive days of success.

Tip: In order for this intervention to be effective, your child must know how to use anger management skills (coping and problem-solving skills). This knowledge and ability takes regular practice. This means you need to set aside time to discuss anger management techniques and to arrange role-play scenarios with your child.

8. Provide small boxes labeled with feelings such as mad, happy, sad, worried, frustrated, and scared. Your child can put an agreed upon item (such as a small stuffed animal or a toy) in the box that corresponds with their feelings at the moment. This will allow you to know how your child is feeling without asking.

   You can also use this system to recognize your child's feelings to show that you are paying attention and want to help. Sometimes, just recognizing your child's feelings is enough to get your child talking.

9. For young children, create an anger hat together. This can be made out of paper, fabric, or whatever other material you can be creative with! When your child places it on their head, everyone needs to leave them alone. This means no one should look, go near, talk to, or bother your child until the hat is put away.

10. Regularly catch your child using positive behavior and tell them what specifically makes you proud.

11. Encourage your child to participate in daily physical activity. This helps them to work through strong emotions, and it may be responsible for helping the brain improve its processing and problem-solving abilities.

12. Always show interest in your child's school and social activities. This shows your child that you care and are willing to take the time to be part of their life.

13. Regularly encourage your child to focus their energy on taking control of their choices. Empowering children to make choices to achieve what they want in life is extremely valuable. With this skill, they can move beyond just focusing on consequences linked to their behavior to considering the outcomes that they are choosing based on their decisions.

14. Develop a plan with your child where you both agree on nonverbal signals that indicate their needs when frustration or anger is being felt. When a corresponding signal is used, your child can then engage in agreed upon activities or can go to a quiet place to deal with their feelings. Be sure that the development of this plan occurs when your child is calm.

15. Once an episode of anger has subsided and your child is calm, give encouragement to state their feelings, accept their feelings, and discover the primary feeling or cause. Ask them what they can do if it happens again. Also, ask what can be done now about the situation.

Counselor's Corner

The Primary Feeling...Discovered

Wondering how to find the primary emotion that your child is displaying? Ask yourself, "What need is not being met?", "What goal is being blocked?"

Examples could include your child not getting their way and feeling jealous that their siblings got to do what your child wanted. Or maybe your child wants to spend time with you but you are in the middle of making dinner so they feel sad and lonely.

Anger is a secondary emotion triggered by other feelings and events.

Put your detective hat on and get to it!

16. It will do you and your family good to remember that all behavior has meaning. The behaviors that your children show reflect a need or a want. If your child is crying, perhaps their need is to get some sleep. If your child is moody, maybe they had a tough day with their peers and could use some support. If your child is staying close, maybe they feel insecure and are longing for your attention and reassurance. Whatever the behavior, be ready to assess it in order to understand what is going on with your children.

17. When planning for future positive decisions, role-play with your child so they have a chance to practice and to become fully prepared.

18. Show confidence in your child's ability to problem-solve. Provide them with supportive planning and practice. Giving your support and confidence will help them learn how to solve problems appropriately.

19. Be the positive role model that your child needs to teach them how to manage emotions and how to get their needs met. If you are a positive role model, much of the teaching will be done just by your child observing you in daily life. Children watch our every move as they figure things out. Let them see how you want them to behave.

20. Teach your child that becoming angry does not solve problems. Encourage them to follow these problem solving steps:

    • Identify the problem.
    • Develop a list of solutions.
    • List the pros and cons for each solution.
    • Pick the best solution.
    • Evaluate. If the solution did not work, pick the next best one.

21. Help your child express angry feelings by using their words (I feel ____ when _____. I need_____).
22. Encourage your child to refocus their energies on something that is enjoyable in order to calm down or to prevent from becoming angry.
23. Use visuals to help redirect your child when becoming frustrated so that the amount of verbal words used are as few as possible. Talking too much to a child can quickly create an overwhelming situation.
24. Help your child to become aware of their rights and the rights of others.
25. Teach your child conflict resolution skills, assertiveness skills, problem-solving skills, and stress management techniques.
26. Involve your child's teacher in the behavior program that you are using at home to help skills transfer into other settings of your child's day.
27. Always be patient as children will need regular reminders of their choices.
28. Visit behaviorcorner.com for more information and contact options for getting additional guidance from a professional therapist.

Anxiety

Introduction

Anxiety can affect a child's thinking, decision-making ability, learning, concentration, and perception of their environment. It raises blood pressure, heart rate, and can cause many physical complaints.

Observable behaviors commonly include: tearfulness, fears, attempting to avoid certain situations, frequently asking for reassurance, being overly cautious, and physical symptoms such as stomachaches and headaches.

Some anxiety is normal and is an expected part of life. However, anxiety becomes a problem when it regularly interrupts normal activities like attending school, making friends, or sleeping. If this becomes the case, an anxiety disorder may be to blame.

Thoughts, actions, and physical symptoms work together to produce anxiety. The ways in which situations are interpreted will result in feeling anxious or not. For example, one person may hear a noise in the middle of the night

> ### Counselor's Corner
> Encourage courage.
>
> Seeing your child struggle with anxiety symptoms is hard to accept. It is normal to want to protect your child and ease their symptoms. However, taking care of things for them and allowing avoidance to ease the symptoms is only a short-term fix and is actually creating a larger anxiety response in the future.
>
> - With your presence, encourage your child to face their fears.
> - Reassure them that you will be with them.
> - Take small steps and acknowledge your child's accomplishments.
>
> Frequently facing one fearful step at a time will build courage and confidence over time; especially when provided with plenty of loving support.

and may interpret it as normal noises of their house and go back to sleep. Another person may hear the same noise and worry that it is an intruder resulting in worry and loss of sleep. As you can see, the same situation can have very different outcomes depending on a person's thoughts, feelings, and behavior.

Anxious individuals tend to interpret situations as threatening or dangerous more often than nonanxious people. Your anxious child will likely need assurance that they are safe in various situations.

The physical symptoms of an anxiety disorder (racing heart, shallow and quick breathing, headaches, nervousness) occur easily even in harmless situations. When these symptoms are present, we see a negative impact in daily functioning, especially when they are experienced unnecessarily.

When experiencing anxious thoughts and heightened physical symptoms, it is natural to want to escape or avoid a situation. It is also very common for an anxious person to try to internally control a fearful situation by asking trusted people for reassurance, being overly cautious, checking to make sure everything is safe, and only focusing on the anxiety.

There are no known causes for anxiety. However, research shows that there are risk factors that may contribute to the development of childhood anxiety. These include the following:

- genetics
- ongoing environmental stressors
- learned behavior from watching or listening to the fears of others
- health issues
- seeing violence or scary scenes on television or in movies
- being parented by someone who is emotional, fearful, high-strung, or overly sensitive

The most effective treatment is provided through a combination of medication and counseling. To easily find a counselor in your area, ask your child's pediatrician for local referrals. Your child's school counselor or school social worker will also be able to provide you with community resources. When you call to make the initial appointment, inquire as to the counselor's specialties to ensure a good fit of care for your child and family.

Formal Diagnosis

Formal diagnoses for specific anxiety disorders are listed in each corresponding section of this chapter.

Interventions

1. Look for warning signs of an anxious child such as

    • frequent physical complaints such as stomachaches, racing heart, etc.;
    • appearing on edge or feeling restless;
    • having poor school attendance;
    • reluctance to leave the home for activities;
    • requests to always be near a caregiver even to the point of not wanting to be in a different room when at home;
    • asking many questions to gain reassurance;
    • consumed with thoughts, images, or actions related to an anxiety trigger;
    • fear over leaving caregivers;
    • fear that something terrible will happen to caregivers when separated;
    • complaining of illness with no medical explanation;
    • having a difficult time sleeping at night, especially without a cosleeping caregiver;
    • easily tired;
    • clinging to caregivers frequently;
    • regular avoidance of anxiety-provoking situations or items;
    • muscle tension;
    • seeming lost in thought about worries;
    • being overly sensitive or emotional;

- frequent nightmares;
- inability to control fears; and
- worries and/or fears significantly impair daily functioning.

A true anxiety disorder may be present when one or more of these symptoms regularly occur on more days than not during consecutive weeks. A medical doctor or a mental health therapist can give an accurate diagnosis after an evaluation of your child, their symptoms, and of the presenting situation(s).

2. Allow your child to see a mental health professional. Therapy can move at your child's pace to explore anxiety symptoms. Most importantly, it is structured, undisturbed time to learn and practice effective ways to manage anxiety.

3. Consider attending family therapy. Many areas of need can be addressed. Finding out how you and others may be unintentionally reinforcing anxiety in your child, learning how to support your child in coping with anxiety, and finding support for yourself are just a few.

4. Contact your child's doctor about your child's anxiety and the anxious behaviors that you are observing. This information is very important to the global care that your child needs from you, their doctor, and a mental health professional in order to treat their anxiety.

5. Don't let a medical or mental health professional's help scare you. Unless your child is in desperate need of care (is suicidal, or harming themselves or others), you have the final say in what treatment is given to your child. Seeking out advice and learning about treatment options is the responsible first step that you should take as a parent. Permission for implementing these plans remains with you.

6. Visit the counselors corner at behaviorcorner.com to arrange for online counseling for you and your child.

7. If you have a teenager, be aware that teens sometimes turn to drugs and/or alcohol to self-medicate in order to escape persistent anxiety. If this is the case, get help for your child immediately.

8. Do not expose your children to violence. This means violence in movies, on television, in video games, and in your home. Children's brains are not developed enough to cope with these events until late adolescence. Prior to this age, children are unable to completely understand the difference between what events are reality and what events are fantasy.

   Children who have anxiety experience even more difficulty processing and coping with violence. They may fear that the violence will happen to them.

   Children also tend to act out what they see especially when it is accepted in their home.

Counselor's Corner
True story...

I remember the child who ended up in my office talking about poor decisions that he had made while in school. It turns out he was bulling a classmate and even went as far as to hit this other boy. I was very surprised because this particular client was not known for violence.

During our discussion, my client said, "I think I have been playing too many video games." This was his own rational as to why his behavior had been so poor lately.

Out of the mouth of babes, huh?

Accepted violence of any kind in the home can have a very negative impact on children's functioning and level of anxiety. Violence has no place when raising healthy kids.

9. Visit the Anxiety and Depression Association of America's website to gain additional supports and information specific to your child's potential condition at www.adaa.org

10. Communicate your child's needs to their teacher(s) and be their advocate. Anxious children may take school requirements and responsibilities more seriously than other students and become upset if they cannot meet them. On the

other hand, it is also common for children who suffer from anxiety to experience school refusal. Communicating your child's needs and developing a school plan will help them to feel more comfortable. (See the School Refusal section in this chapter for additional tips.)

11. Be accepting of less than perfect achievements from yourself and from your child. When you make a mistake or fall short of meeting a goal, make your plan known of how you are going to do things differently next time. By doing this, you are serving as a role model on how to deal with imperfections.

12. Understand that young children cannot fully comprehend the concept of intentional avoidance. What they do understand though is that they feel upset and worried by something and they don't want to have those feelings again. Be understanding and supportive that your child may not be displaying challenging behaviors to be defiant; it is simply a reaction to strong emotions.

13. Decrease the use of stimulants when possible. Stimulants are found in caffeine, asthma medications, and cough medications.

14. Provide your child with daily downtime to allow for relaxation and to process any anxious thoughts with you.

15. Remind your child and yourself that normal fear occurs when danger is a reality. Anxiety occurs when danger *might* occur. An older child should be able to process the difference in order to help sort through unnecessary anxiety symptoms.

16. Don't force your child to confront their fear directly. Take it slowly—one step at a time. Give encouragement along the way. Breaking down large tasks and facing fears slowly helps to ease anxiety symptoms. No matter how small the step taken, tell your child how proud you are of them. Next time, a further step can be taken. Do not become

frustrated during this process as that will deter your child from trying again in the future.

17. Pay attention to your own reactions and problem-solving abilities. The ways in which people think, feel, and behave in situations of perceived threat can increase or decrease their anxiety. Your children will observe your daily actions and will likely follow your example.

18. Talk with your child about how they feel. Expressing their feelings can help them feel more in control and supported.

19. For young children, pretend through use of toys or puppets to understand what is bothering them. Problem-solving can also take place through this method. Children will be more apt to express themselves through means of the toy or puppet instead of speaking directly about the issues. Pretending that an issue is the toy's problem makes it easier for kids to communicate their thoughts and feelings.

20. Use drawings or art supplies to help your child express their thoughts, feelings, and worries. This can be a more comfortable way for your child to share what is inside.

21. Blow bubbles to teach deep breathing. Guide your child in blowing big bubbles with a bubble wand. To do this, your child needs to be relaxed enough to be successful.

22. Use a calm approach when supporting your child though times of anxiety. Anxiety can be influenced in either direction by the reactions and responses given by caregivers.

23. Try your best to not be hurried. Parents who are in a rush have less time to be proactive, positive, and preventative.

Counselor's Corner

I could go on and on about the number of times I have rushed my family out the door, around town, or to bed. Modern living demands that we use multitasking behaviors and make the most of every minute. Hence, the texting, phone calls, wireless connections, speeding tickets, over-booked schedules and so on.

Take your life back and renew your sanity. To do this, make a plan and stick to it. Plan for what your family can handle and no more. This plan should include activities that your children **want** to do as well as the things that you **need** to do. Prioritize what tasks need to be done and decide which ones can wait. This will help you to avoid racing against the clock to get it all done.

Put the cell phone down. Kids tell me all the time that all their parents do is text, talk on the phone or use the computer. How frustrating it must be for these children. Even if you think they don't mind...I assure you they do. They want to be with you! They want to be the center of your world. Show them how important they are to you by putting the technology aside.

Spending time with your children is much more important than checking everything off of your list or sending just one more text.

24. Teach calming and problem-solving skills to help your child remain calm. Teaching children how to deal with anxiety instead of running from it generally results in overcoming fears and worries. Be proactive and willing to support your child through this process. See appendix B for ideas.

25. Provide a consistent routine for your child at home and in other areas of the day. Children who know what to expect and who are given plenty of notice when things need to change feel more in control and seem to have less anxious days. A consistent routine even helps children to sleep better at night.

26. Do not tell your child to calm down. They wish that they could relax. They don't need you saying it; they need you to teach it and model it.

27. Help your child learn coping skills to manage anxiety symptoms. Some common ways to calm the body include

- deep breathing (inhale to the count of three, hold to the count of three, exhale to the count of three, repeat);
- counting;
- visualizing a calm and happy place; and
- positive self-talk ("I know I will be okay," or "I can handle this").

For further coping ideas, see appendix B.

28. Do not predict future conflict or fear for your child. "Rescuing" children without allowing for problem-solving can create anxious and dependent behavior. Equip your child with coping strategies (appendix B) to tackle situations independently.

29. Boys do best with physical coping strategies such as deep breathing and exercising. Girls do best with mental techniques such as visualizing a peaceful place. Be willing to cater to your child's needs by being creative and flexible in trying new strategies.

30. Do not tell your child to stop crying or that there is nothing to worry about. This causes them to feel unsupported. Their fears are very real to them. Tell them it is okay to cry. Work with your child frequently to problem-solve and to cope with their anxiety.

31. Never make fun of your child's fears or worries. To your child, their worries are very real and not at all funny.

32. Role-play. Brainstorm possible solutions to situations and then act them out. Adding the acting element further solidifies the skill and increases your child's confidence.

33. Promote quiet routines in your home.

34. Maintain a calm, safe, and supportive home.

35. Listen to your child's fears without judging them negatively. Ask the following questions to help them think about their fears in a rational way:

- What proof do you have that your worry/fear will come true?
- Is this always the case?
- Has this happened in the past?
- What is the worst thing that could happen?
- What would you do if it the worst happened?

36. Read books about children facing their fears to help them learn coping strategies and to start conversations about your child's own fears. My suggestions include the following:

    1. Books to read *with* your kids

       a. *Is a Worry Worrying You?* By Ferida Wolff and Harriet May Savitz
       b. *Sometimes I Worry Too Much but Now I Know How to Stop: A Book to Help Children Who Worry When They Don't Need To* By Dawn A. Huebner, PhD
       c. *What to Do When You're Scared and Worried* By: James J. Crist, PhD
       d. *I Don't Want to Go to School: Helping Children Cope with Separation Anxiety* By Nancy Pando, LICSW

    2. Workbooks for you and your child to do *together*

       a. *I Bet...I Won't Fret: A Workbook That Helps Kids Beat the Worries* By Timothy A. Sisemore
       b. *What to Do When You Worry Too Much: A Kid's Guide to Overcoming Anxiety* By Dawn Huebner, PhD

3. Resource book for parents

    a. *Worried No More: Help and Hope for Anxious Children Second Edition* By Aureen Pinto Wagner, PhD

37. Create a personal coping box that contains items that will help your child to feel calm and to think happy thoughts. Paste coping skill steps to the lid to remind them of the steps to take when feeling anxious. Use pictures if needed to help your child remember the steps. While they are using their calming/happy items, the coping skill steps should be used. Regularly review and practice how to use the coping box together.

38. Try not to give reassurances to your child that everything will be okay. This dismisses the worry that they are experiencing. Additionally, your child is smart enough to know that things don't always turn out okay. Making promises in some situations where you don't have complete control may end up doing the opposite of what you intended.

39. Your child must understand and accept that they have the power to solve their own problems. Of course, they will have your support in beating their worries, but they have to be the one to use the strategies. Once your child has obtained control by using skills to overcome anxiety, the anxiety will have less power.

40. Set goals and track progress through journaling or other visual means that can be reflected upon. If your child is too young or overwhelmed for journaling, you can write their thoughts and progress for them.

It is helpful to have agreed upon weekly tasks or goals written directly into the journal with an empty box next to each one for your child to check off as they complete their tasks or goals. These tasks or goals need to be directly related to coping with the presenting anxiety situation(s).

Tip: An alternative to this is placing a blank line next to each task or goal for your child to rate their level of anxiety on a scale of 0 to 10. The number indicated on the line shows how anxious your child felt while completing the task or goal. Not only is this good for progress monitoring, but it also lends itself to helpful conversations.

41. Consider your child's abilities when expecting certain behaviors or expectations. If you feel your child should be able to meet your expectations, spend some time practicing what needs to be done so that they feel more confident instead of worried.

42. Do not be an overprotective parent. Allow your child to learn from their own mistakes. Allow them to experience this world with some freedom and independence. Being overprotective fosters anxiety in children that normally would not occur on its own. For example, if you express worry that your child may get bullied while riding the school bus, they will most likely fear this activity just like you do. Give your child a chance to break the cycle of anxiety.

43. Do not continue to ask your child why they feel anxious. Frequently, children are not able to identify a solid reason.

44. Provide your child with reassurance of your love for them. Children who experience anxiety can display behaviors ranging from quiet all the way to angry. Children process their feelings of anxiety in different ways. Despite how your child reacts to their feelings, support them by teaching how to effectively work through their symptoms. Above all, regularly tell your child that you love them no matter what!

45. Visit behaviorcorner.com for more information and contact options for getting additional guidance from a professional therapist.

Bonus: On-the-Spot Interventions

1. For an on-the-spot anxiety reducer, give your child a cold glass of water to drink. This quickly decreases their fast heart rate. In between swallows, tell your child to breathe deeply and to visualize their heart slowing to a normal beat.

2. Deep breathing helps to promote relaxation. Guide your child through this process by teaching them to

    1. inhale through their nose slowly while counting to three;
    2. pause and hold their breath until the count of three;
    3. exhale slowly to a count of three (exhale fully);
    4. take two normal breaths; and
    5. repeat for three to five minutes.

    When doing this with young kids, tell them to make a humming sound when exhaling. This helps with focusing on their breathing and makes it a bit more fun.

3. Show your child how to inhale slowly to a count of three. Tell them to imagine their breath coming in slowly through their nose and down into their lungs. While exhaling, guide them to relax their muscles and imagine their breath coming up from the lungs and out their mouth.

4. Brainstorm a calm place that your child has been before. Encourage them to remember the tastes, sights, and sounds of this place. All of these things will enhance the calming experience.

    When beginning to feel anxiety, remind your child of their calming place and support them in remembering all the traits of this place.

5. Give your child time. Wait with them when their anxiety is high. This can be reassuring because they can see that they don't have to do anything except wait. Anxious feel-

ings typically increase and then will eventually decrease on their own over time.

Specific Anxiety Concerns

Generalized anxiety disorder, separation anxiety disorder, phobias, school refusal, and *social anxiety disorder* are some common phrases heard when speaking about childhood anxiety. Each of these will be explored in the pages ahead.

Each situation and person is different. That said, be flexible in your expectations. Give a strategy or two a try and be willing to tweak things as you go. When trying to manage specific anxiety concerns, give the following disorder-specific interventions a try as a nice compliment to strategies already in place.

Generalized Anxiety Disorder

Introduction

Let's be honest; we have all experienced anxiety in our lives. Anxiety is normal and is part of being human. However, some of us humans are more prone to experiencing anxiety than others. Thoughts, situations, and people can all cause us to feel anxious at one time or another. The way in which we interpret these thoughts, situations, and people will determine if anxiety will be felt.

Healthy and helpful anxiety has a main purpose to keep us away from danger, and in some cases, anxiety guides us in selecting right from wrong. As much as anxiety can be a positive influence, it can be even more so of a burden when its presence is not helping us stay safe or is not guiding our decision-making process. Generalized anxiety disorder (GAD) is well known for this anxious burden.

In my experience, adults who encounter regular feelings of anxiety in their daily functioning can typically identify reasons for the anxiety and can state that they logically know that their anxious feelings have no merit. Despite this acknowledgement, the anxiety still occurs until the person finds treatment.

In children, GAD causes the child to feel nervous most days. Depending on the child's age, identifying a reason why they are feeling anxious can be difficult or even impossible. This causes the child to live in a heightened state of awareness, unhappiness, and worry. As you can image, their overall functioning from day to day becomes impacted. This may include their decline in their school grades, strained relationships, sleep interruptions, forgetfulness, and/or changes in their behavior.

Additionally, children with GAD are usually eager to please and can be viewed as "perfectionists." They may become frustrated and dissatisfied with less-than-perfect results. Seeking approval and constant reassurance from others about their performance and anxieties is very common. This type of behavior proves to be very time-consuming and may cause frustration for the children and caregivers.

Formal Diagnosis

Generalized anxiety disorder (GAD) is described by the American Psychiatric Association as excessive anxiety and worry about a number of events or activities. These anxieties and worries are difficult to control and must be experienced during more days than not for at least six months. During this six-month time, at least one of the following must be present in children for a diagnosis:

Common Co-Existing Conditions

- Depression
- Low self-esteem
- Additional anxiety disorders
- Attention-deficit/hyperactivity disorder
- Substance use
- Medical conditions

- feeling restless, keyed up, or on edge
- becoming easily tired

- difficulty concentrating or their mind goes blank
- irritability
- muscle tension
- sleep problems such as difficulty with falling asleep, staying asleep, or having restless unsatisfying sleep

The anxiety, worry, or symptom(s) must have a negative impact on the child's daily functioning to meet the diagnostic criteria of GAD. Additionally, the symptoms cannot be better accounted for by another mental disorder or medical condition.

Common anxieties and worries for children with GAD include

- getting good grades in school,
- sports performance,
- natural disasters,
- war, and
- pleasing others.

The strategies listed earlier for easing overall anxiety symptoms can be effective for children who experience GAD. However, the following have been researched to be the best matches in treating generalize anxiety disorder. Many of these have also been included earlier.

Interventions

1. Learn about your child's anxiety disorder and what it means for them and your family. Speak with your child's doctor and seek out the support from a mental health professional when looking for this information. They are two great places to start.
2. Visit the Counselor's Corner at behaviorcorner.com to arrange for online counseling for you and your child.
3. Don't let a medical or mental health professional's help scare you. Unless your child is in desperate need of care (is suicidal, or harming themself), you have the final say in

what treatment is given to your child. Seeking out advice and learning about treatment options is the responsible first step that you should take as a parent. Permission for implementing these plans remains with you.

4. Strive to keep your child's mental health appointments each time they are scheduled. Therapy can move at your child's pace to explore anxiety symptoms. Most importantly, it is structured, undisturbed time to learn and practice effective ways to manage anxiety.

5. Consider attending family therapy. Many areas of need can be addressed. Finding out how you and others may be unintentionally reinforcing anxiety in your child, learning how to support your child in coping with anxiety, and finding support for yourself are only a few.

6. Encourage your child to journal. If they refuse, you can record what they tell you. Write down daily fears, thoughts, and any coping skills that were used. Reflection on these can be very powerful in allowing your child to see that they can handle situations. Coping skills can be found by visiting appendix B.

   Many times, when reviewing the journal, children will not remember why they were worried about a situation in the first place. Use this as a learning experience to lovingly point out that worry was unnecessary since they can't remember what caused their anxious feelings.

7. Do not continue to ask your child why they feel anxious. Frequently, children are not able to identify a solid reason.

8. Help your child learn coping skills to manage anxiety symptoms. Some common ways to calm the body include the following:

   • deep breathing (inhale to the count of three, hold to the count of three, exhale to the count of three, repeat)
   • counting
   • visualizing a calm and happy place

- positive self-talk ("I know I will be okay" or "I can handle this")

9. Help your child build their problem-solving abilities. Do this through brainstorming possible solutions to situations and then acting them out. Adding the acting element further solidifies the skill and increases your child's confidence. If you need further guidance, contact a medical or mental health professional.

   To get you started, ask your child's doctor or the school counselor/school social worker at your child's school for referrals to mental health counselors in your area. Prior to scheduling your child's first appointment, call to inquire about the counselor's specialty and to get a sense if they will be a good fit for your child.

10. Communicate regularly with your child's teacher. It is common for children who suffer from generalized anxiety disorder to also experience school refusal. Communicating your child's needs and making a plan will help your child feel more comfortable. (See the School Refusal section of this chapter for additional tips.)

11. Provide your child with reassurance of your love for them. Children who experience anxiety can display behaviors ranging from quiet all the way to angry. Children process their feelings of anxiety in different ways. Despite how your child reacts to their feelings, support them by teaching how to effectively work through their symptoms. Above all, regularly tell your child that you love them no matter what!

12. Provide a consistent routine for your child at home and in other areas of their day. Children who know what to expect and who are given plenty of notice of changes of the day's events feel more in control and seem to have less anxious days. A consistent routine even helps children to sleep better at night.

13. Never make fun of your child's fears or worries. To your child, their worries are very real and not at all funny.
14. Consider your child's abilities when expecting certain behaviors or expectations. If you feel your child should be able to meet your expectations, spend some time practicing what needs to be done so they feel more confident instead of worried.
15. Encourage participation in daily activities. Celebrate successes made during these activities, no matter how small.
16. Be proactive by giving opportunities for your child to discover that there is nothing to worry about. For example, if your child experiences anxiety prior to a new school year beginning, arrange a step-by-step plan to expose them to the situation.

    For example: arrange for a tour of the school to reintroduce your child to their surroundings. While there, your child can see where their new classroom will be. Follow this up with a meeting between the teacher, you, and your child. Lastly, request a visit that will allow your child to bring in their school supplies and to get organized for the new school year. Breaking this down into a step-by-step process allows your child to take it slow while being exposed to a little more of the anxiety-producing situation each time. This will greatly ease anxiety come day one of school.

    Reassure your child every step of the way that you are with them. At the end, give praise for success made (even if it was just riding in the car to get to the school's parking lot).
17. Do not tell your child to calm down. They wish that they could relax. They don't need you saying it; they need you to teach it and model it.
18. Talk with your child about how they feel. Expressing their feelings can help them feel more in control and supported.

19. Be accepting of less than perfect achievements from yourself and your child. When you make a mistake or fall short of meeting a goal, make your plan known of how you are going to do things differently next time. By doing this, you are serving as a role model on how to deal with imperfections.

> No one is perfect and that is okay! Change takes planning, time, and patience.

20. Use drawings or art supplies to help your child express their thoughts, feelings, and worries. This can be a more comfortable way for your child to share what is inside.

21. Take it step-by-step and give encouragement along the way. Breaking down large tasks and facing fears slowly helps to ease anxiety symptoms. No matter how small the step taken, tell your child how proud you are of them. Next time, a further step can be taken. Do not become frustrated during this process as that will deter your child from trying again in the future.

22. Do not expose your children to violence. This means violence in movies, on television, in video games, and in your home. Children's brains are not developed enough to cope with these events until late adolescence. Prior to late adolescence, children are unable to completely understand the difference between events that are reality and events that are fantasy.

    Children who have anxiety experience even more difficulty processing and coping with violence. They may fear that the violence will happen to them. Children also tend to act out what they see, especially when it is accepted in their home.

23. Visit behaviorcorner.com for more information and contact options for getting additional guidance from a professional therapist.

Separation Anxiety Disorder

Introduction

Separation anxiety disorder occurs when intense anxiety is felt about being away from home or away from those whom the child is attached. It is normal for very young children to experience separation anxiety. However, when children continue to experience separation anxiety symptoms as they age and when their daily life is negatively impacted because of it, a true case of separation anxiety disorder may be to blame.

Formal Diagnosis

According to the American Psychiatry Association, separation anxiety disorder is identified when developmentally inappropriate and excessive fear is experienced over the separation from those to whom the individual is attached. This is shown by the person showing at least three of the following:

- repeated and excessive distress when expecting or experiencing separation from home or from major attachment figures
- persistent and excessive worry about losing a major attachment figure or about possible harm happening to them
- persistent and excessive worry that something bad will happen, resulting in the separation from a major attachment figure

Common Co-Existing Conditions

- Specific phobia(s)
- Mood disorders
- Enuresis
- Additional anxiety disorders
- Depression
- School refusal
- Suicide risk
- Substance use

- persistent unwillingness or refusal to go to school or elsewhere because of the fear of separation
- persistently and excessively fearing or showing unwillingness to be alone or without major attachment figures at home or in other settings (children may not even want their caregiver to leave the room that they are sharing)
- persistent reluctance or refusal to sleep away from home or to go to sleep without being near a major attachment figure
- repeated nightmares involving the theme of separation
- repeated complaints of physical symptoms (stomachaches, headaches, vomiting) when separation from major attachment figures occurs or is expected

The symptoms must last for at least four weeks in children and must result in distress or significant impairment in the child's daily functioning to meet the criteria for separation anxiety. Lastly, the symptoms cannot be better explained by another mental disorder.

Separation anxiety symptoms commonly present themselves in different ways depending on the age of the child. The following are behaviors that are commonly seen in children diagnosed with separation anxiety disorder:

- Children eight years of age and younger may have unfounded fears or worries about harm happening to their caregivers, fear of the dark, and monsters, etc. They may also have several physical illness complaints.
- Children nine through twelve years of age may display severe distress during times of separation such as withdrawal, sadness, or difficulty concentrating. Physical complaints about not feeling well are also common.
- Children twelve through sixteen years of age are most likely to present with separation anxiety symptoms when trying to adjust with life changes such as a parents' divorce, a family trauma, or attending a new school.

They are typically reluctant to leave their caregiver's side even to go to familiar places. Physical symptoms are also common such as headaches, stomachaches, fatigue, a racing heart, etc.

Children who have separation anxiety disorder can present as needy and demanding of their caregiver's time. They need a lot of attention and may even show anger and aggression at the thought of having to separate from major attachment figures.

The most effective interventions appear to be based in behavior planning and medication management. The following interventions will help to support your behavior plans to guide your child through this difficult time.

Interventions

1. Allow your child to see a mental health professional. Therapy can move at your child's pace to explore separation anxiety symptoms. Most importantly, it is structured, undisturbed time to learn and practice effective ways to manage this anxiety.
2. Consider attending family therapy. Many areas of need can be addressed. Finding out how you and others may be unintentionally reinforcing separation anxiety in your child, learning how to support your child in coping with separation anxiety, and finding support for yourself are just a few of the many benefits.
3. Contact your child's doctor to make them aware of your child's anxiety concerns and related behaviors. They are part of the team that will help your child overcome this difficult time.
4. Don't let a medical or mental health professional's help scare you. Unless your child is in desperate need of care (is suicidal, or harming themselves or others), you have the final say in what treatment is given to your child.

Seeking out advice and learning about treatment options is the responsible first step that you should take as a parent. Permission for implementing these plans remains with you.

5. Visit the Counselor's Corner at behaviorcorner.com to arrange for online counseling for you and your child.

6. Insist that your child attends school. It is common for separation anxiety to include school refusal. Anxiety in this case is usually over the act of leaving home, so once your child is in school, their anxiety will frequently decrease after a short time.

> When kids start to understand that the worst that can happen really isn't that bad, power is taken away from the anxiety and they begin to reclaim their life again.

7. Talk with your child and with school staff to identify worries that are associated with attending school and about leaving you or other caregivers. Lovingly challenge your child's irrational fears and create a plan to increase the amount of time spent in school. Ask your child the following questions:

    •   "What is the worst that will happen?"
    •   "What are the chances of it happening?"
    •   "What can some of the solutions be in that case?"

    Your child will feel that their worries are supported, yet those worries don't deserve all the energy that they are spending on them.

8. Develop coping strategies such as deep breathing, thinking happy thoughts, positive self-statements, and a reward program. See appendix A and B for ideas.

9. Acknowledge that the distress being felt by your child is real. Develop a plan to help them cope. See appendix A and appendix B for ideas.

10. Create a goal. Break the goal into small steps that your child can work toward. Begin with the step that causes the least amount of anxiety. Make each step a bit more challenging than the last.

    It is most helpful to have your child visualize being successful with each step, making a plan of action, and then actually doing it.

    See the social anxiety disorder section of this chapter for an example of this step-by-step process.

11. Frequently review and practice your child's coping skills and reflect on successes made.

12. Regularly reflect on how your child's plan and coping skills are working. Make any necessary changes.

13. When your child has to leave you, assign a special job for them to do while you two are apart. This results in your child feeling like they have a purpose and can focus on that job instead of just the issue of separation. When you return, you can tell them how proud you are of the job they did.

14. Encourage your child to engage in playdates with peers. Begin by having a peer come to your home and then set up a time for your child to go to that friend's house for the next playdate.

    Be sure that the adult in the friend's home is aware of your child's needs. Put a plan in place for the time that your child is spending there. This will help to reassure your child and will allow the friend's parents to have the answers for potential separation anxiety issues.

15. It is common for separation anxiety to begin or increase after a trauma, illness, a break from school, or a change in the family. Be especially patient and supportive during these times. Given the right amount of support, separation anxiety will be a temporary issue for your child.

16. Visit behaviorcorner.com for more information and contact options for getting additional guidance from a professional therapist.

School Refusal

Introduction

School refusal exists when your child refuses to go to school. When this happens, your first action must be to work with the school and also with your child's pediatrician.

The most common reasons for school refusal are not wanting to leave caregivers (commonly termed as separation anxiety) and having worries about something at school. Examples could include anxiety over peer interactions or worries about undesirable things happening while in school.

For example, I have seen a few children who were worried about other students vomiting while in school. Their worry over this presented as a concern over germs, getting sick themselves, and worry over the embarrassment for that student. This worry made coming to school every day very difficult for these students.

Whatever the reason and however rational or not, there are steps you can take to get your child back to school and their anxiety under control.

Formal Diagnosis

School refusal is not a recognized diagnosis by the American Psychiatric Association. However, school refusal can be a common symptom of the anxiety disorders presented here.

Interventions

1. Allow your child to see the school counselor. If concerns continue, seeking the additional help of a mental health profes-

sional is recommended. School counselors and mental health counselors can work together to help your child succeed

2. Visit the Counselor's Corner at behaviorcorner.com to arrange for online counseling for you and your child.

3. Develop a plan with the school. Some helpful ideas include setting up a different mode of transportation (taking the bus, walking, or getting a ride with a friend or relative), implementing an incentive plan for attending school, and requesting a support staff member to work with your child each morning and as needed throughout the day until the anxiety subsides.

4. Develop coping strategies with your child such as deep breathing, thinking happy thoughts, positive self-statements, and a reward program. See appendix A and B for further ideas.

5. Talk with your child and with school staff to identify worries that are associated with attending school and about leaving you or other caregivers. Lovingly challenge your child's irrational fears and create a plan to increase the amount of time spent in school. Ask your child the following questions:

   • "What is the worst that will happen?"
   • "What are the chances of it happening?"
   • "What can some of the solutions be in that case?"

   Your child will feel that their worries are supported, and will see that those worries don't deserve all the energy that they are spending on them.

6. If your child stays home (and is not sick), do not allow them to have any fun or privileges while home. They must stay in their room and only read books for school or do homework.

7. Give acknowledgement and rewards for attending school and all other steps taken toward that goal such as getting out of bed, getting ready, eating breakfast, etc.
8. If your child's goal is to gain attention from their attempts to refuse school, ignore the behavior and carry on through the morning routine.
9. Return your child to school as soon as possible and stick to your family's normal routine.
10. For extreme cases, bring your child to school for the last thirty minutes of each day. Gradually increase the amount of time your child attends school. Looking forward to the end of the school day gives anxious children an incentive to attend.
11. You must get your child to school each day. Have a school staff member meet you if needed to take your child. Give praise for the time spent in school and positive choices that you child made throughout the day.
12. Visit behaviorcorner.com for more information and contact options for getting additional guidance from a professional therapist.

Phobias

Introduction

Fear in general is a normal human reaction. Healthy fear serves us well to keep us safe from dangerous situations. It is when our irrational fears inhibit our daily actions that it becomes a problem. For example, if one fears dogs and avoids going places where a dog might be, that person is allowing fear to greatly hinder life decisions. This is an example of a phobia.

Phobias are things that cause intense fear despite real danger being a small or nonexistent threat.

When thinking about an identified fear, the phobic person may feel uneasy yet reassured by the fact that they are not exposed to the fear at that time. However, when faced directly with the fear, the person experiences overwhelming distress and looks for escape or safety from the situation. Future attempts to avoid the situation are typically made but come with a large inconvenience to the phobic person and to family members.

Symptoms that occur when faced with thoughts or with the presence of a phobic situation include the following possibilities:

- racing heart rate
- rapid breathing
- attempts and/or a strong desire to escape or avoid a situation
- children may cling to caregivers
- sweating
- shaking
- crying
- stomachache or headache
- children may have tantrums
- trouble focusing on anything but the phobia
- feeling unable to control one's fear
- trouble making decisions
- feeling so overwhelmed that the person feels as though they will pass out

It is expected that children will have fears. In fact, it is normal for kids to experience excessive worry or fear at some points of their life. These times are generally short-term and occur infrequently.

Worries and fears are a normal part of growing up. When your child is very young, let's say from their infancy up to three years of age, expect them to be afraid of strangers, new situations, and of caregivers leaving. From ages four to seven, many kids experience fears such as the dark, monsters, thunderstorms, or bees. From ages eight to sixteen, it is common for children to have fears related to violence, death, injury, lack of school success, and the welfare of their friends.

During these times of various worries, talk to your child about their concerns and provide them with reassurance that you love them and that they are safe. Talking through, visually seeing, or experiencing a fear with you by their side may be just the thing they need to see that everything is okay. If you choose to expose your child to their fear, talk about the experience with them before and after the two of you face their fear together. Ask them how they felt, what they were thinking, how they feel now, and rate their level of anxiety as they think about facing their fear again in the future.

Above all, be patient. Normal worries come and go. Some may even stick around for a few weeks. If you remain patient, loving, and supportive, the day will come when the worry isn't even mentioned anymore. Ahhh…success!

As you now know, worries and fears are all very normal experiences of childhood. However, if your child is obsessing over any of these or over different issues for a few months or more and it is negatively impacting their quality of life, seek the advice of your child's doctor or a mental health professional.

> Worries that last for only a short time are a normal part of growing up.

Formal Diagnosis: Specific Phobia

Common Co-Existing Conditions

- Depression
- Additional anxiety disorders
- Bipolar disorder
- Substance use
- Personality disorder

According to the American Psychiatric Association, specific phobia is described below.

• An obvious fear or anxiety about a specific object or situation. In children, this fear or anxiety may be shown through crying, tantrums, freezing, or clinging behavior.

- The phobic object or situation almost always triggers immediate fear or anxiety.

- The individual seeks to avoid the phobic object or situation or endures it with intense fear or anxiety.

- The fear or anxiety is an excessive response to the actual danger being presented by the specific object or situation. It must also be in excess of what is accepted in the person's culture and what social surroundings deem as appropriate.

- The individual's daily life and functioning is negatively impacted by the phobia.

- The phobic response is not better categorized by another mental disorder.

The symptoms of specific phobia must be present for at least six months to receive the diagnosis.

Phobias can develop in a variety of settings and can be trigged by countless things. Due to the commonalities of phobias experienced, subcategories of specific phobias include four areas.

Whether included in one of these subcategories or not, please keep in mind that fears must be negatively impacting one's daily functioning to be considered a phobia. Having fear yet not allowing it to dictate one's choices does not qualify as a true phobia.

- Animal phobia – fear of animals such as dogs, snakes, or spiders

- Natural environment – fear of things such as heights, thunderstorms, water, or sounds

- Blood and injection injury – fear of medical procedures including needles

- Situational – fear that occurs given a particular situation such as being in a forest, driving on a bridge, or flying in an airplane

- Other – fear of choking, vomiting, loud sounds, costumed characters

Interventions

Specific phobias and social anxiety disorder share common interventions. Interventions for both disorders are listed after the introduction and formal diagnosis of social anxiety disorder is presented.

Social Anxiety Disorder

Introduction

People who suffer from social anxiety disorder are known to be overly sensitive to criticism, have trouble being assertive, and suffer from low self-esteem. They typically are afraid of leaving surroundings in which they are comfortable, such as their own home. Going to the store, school, church, or anywhere else where they feel that their actions may be scrutinized are avoided or faced with a large degree of anxiety.

The effects of social anxiety disorder can be seen in a person's overall functioning. Basic needs may not be met if the person can't overcome their fears to interact with others or to buy necessary items from a store. Relationships with family and friends are negatively impacted as one's social anxiety will keep them away from most social outings.

Social anxiety disorder can make people, and especially children, feel very alone. Siblings and peers seem to go about enjoying life while children with social anxiety disorder are unable to join this social developmental time in their life. In addition, attending school is likely to be seen as an unsafe and perhaps a paralyzing place where being social, speaking in front of others, and eating in the cafeteria are expected. Left untreated, social anxiety can lead to other mental disorders lasting into adulthood.

Formal Diagnosis

According to the American Psychiatric Association, social anxiety disorder is diagnosed when the following situations happen:

- An obvious fear or anxiety about one or more social situations in which the person is exposed to possible scrutiny by others. Examples include social interactions (having a conversation), being observed (eating or drinking), and performing in front of others (giving a speech). In children, this response must occur with their peers and not just while interacting with adults.

  Common Co-Existing Conditions

  - Depression
  - Low self-esteem
  - Additional anxiety disorders
  - Substance use
  - Suicide risk
  - High functioning autism
  - Selective mutism
  - Attention-deficit/hyperactivity disorder

- The person fears that they will act in a way or show anxiety symptoms that would be negatively viewed by others.
- Social situations almost always bring on fear or anxiety. In children, the symptoms may be shown through crying, tantrums, freezing, clinging, shrinking, or failing to speak in social situations.
- The feared social situations are avoided or are endured with intense fear or anxiety.
- The fear or anxiety is an excessive response to the actual danger being presented by the specific object or situation. It must also be in excess of what is accepted in that the person's culture and what the social surroundings deem as appropriate
- The person's daily life and functioning is negatively impacted by fear, anxiety, or avoidance.

- The fear, anxiety, or avoidance is not better explained by another mental disorder, a medical condition, or a response to substance use.

The symptoms for social anxiety disorder must be present for at least six months to receive the diagnosis.

Regardless of your child's diagnostic status or type of phobia, these strategies will serve you both well in your quest to effectively manage phobias and social anxiety.

Interventions

1. Arrange for your child to see a mental health professional. Using the following interventions under the guidance of a mental health provider will make them even more effective and help everyone to stay on track.

2. Visit the Counselor's Corner at behaviorcorner.com to arrange for online counseling for you and your child.

3. Contact your child's doctor to consult about your child's phobic or social anxiety responses. A medical professional is a key person that will help in the treatment process.

4. Don't let a medical or mental health professional's help scare you. Unless your child is in desperate need of care (is suicidal, or harming themselves or others), you have the final say in what treatment is given to your child. Seeking out advice and learning about treatment options is the responsible first step that you should take as a parent. Permission for implementing these plans remains with you.

5. Work with your child to honestly identify their fears. Once these fears are acknowledged, work with them to cope and gradually decrease their fearful responses. See appendix B for coping strategies.

    Gradual exposure occurs when you support your child in taking small steps toward full exposure. This process takes time and patience, but it is well worth it. An example includes the following:

1. Begin with talking with your child about the fear.
2. Talk about it again and draw a picture of it.
3. Talk about it again and find a real picture of the fear.
4. Talk about it again and help your child visualize themselves with the anxiety trigger while in the physical safety of their own home.
5. Talk about their anxiety trigger, drawings, pictures, and visualizations. Make plans to gain exposure to part of the anxiety. This could include steps such as riding in the car toward an anxiety provoking place, going to the zoo to see an animal that creates an anxious response, or going the doctor's office. Decide how far your child is willing to go. Are they willing to walk into the zoo, or just stand outside of it? Either way, a step was taken in the right direction. You both should be proud.
6. Talk about steps that were taken. Plan for an additional further step to occur.
7. Continue taking small steps toward the anxiety provoking situation all the while keeping your child safe by your side.

Reward and acknowledge every step taken in this process, no matter how small. At the end of it all, your child may never feel completely comfortable, but they will know that they don't have to let a fear rule their lives.

Counselor's Corner

Exposure steps

Use steps to help your child face their fears in a healthy way. Space these steps out with at least a few days in between each one. When one step has been completed (or just talked about) make plans for when the next step (or the same step) will occur.

*Repeating or failing a step is okay. It is all part of the process. Reward the effort.

6. Perceived danger is reinforced each time a child is allowed to escape or avoid a situation. Work through gradual steps to encourage success in facing their fear. Repeated avoidance only makes the fear more real. If the exposure process is too difficult, get the help of a mental health professional to assist you and your family. Sometimes, having a neutral third party involved makes all the difference.

   Tip: Use a hierarchy to arrange exposure steps from least threatening to most threatening. Start small, such as thinking of the fear. Moving slowly through the steps will help to promote the most success. Each time your child puts forth effort in facing a step, reward them and make it known how proud you are. Also, provide reassurance that you will always support them.

7. Support your child in reinforcing the normalcy of anxiety in the face of fear. Remind them that when overcoming a phobia, they will feel uncomfortable. This is all part of the process.

8. Understand that young children cannot fully comprehend the concept of intentional avoidance. What they do understand though is that they feel upset and worried by something and they don't want to have those feelings again. Be understanding and supportive that your child may not be displaying challenging behaviors to be defiant; it is simply a reaction to strong emotions.

9. Teach your child coping skills and relaxation techniques (see appendix B). It is normal for people to feel anxious when facing their fears, even at the least threatening level. Your child should never feel overwhelmed by emotion while trying to overcome their fear. If they do, consider working through the exposure steps at a slower pace and regularly practice relaxation techniques. Being able to relax one's body helps to decrease the amount of anxiety and fear experienced.

10. Show your child how to remain calm in the face of fear. Your modeling will help them to understand what their choices are. Once you tell your child about a skill and then show them how to use the skill, have your child try it as practice. The more practice they get, the more able they will be to apply the skill in daily life.

11. Be patient and go at your child's pace. Forcing your child to move too fast will create more anxiety.

12. Practice and review coping skills, relaxation techniques, and exposure steps regularly. Do this even when the phobia or anxiety symptoms seem to be manageable. By keeping these important management tools and successes present, the fear has less power and control over your child.

13. Use distraction. When your child begins to feel anxious, teach them to focus on other things such as the color of the shirt that the person next to them is wearing. This will give the brain a break from the fear-causing situation and allow for your child to regroup their composure.

14. Empower your child to take control of the fear. Loss of control is central in phobia and fear. Not being in control of the weather, the actions of others, the actions of an animal, and so on are all things that can make a fearful person feel unsafe due to loss of control. Guiding your child through choices that they have control of along with strategies to keep calm in fear-provoking situations will provide optimism in overcoming their fears.

15. Teach your child to use rational thinking to challenge negative thoughts. For example, if your child has a fear of someone vomiting during class, they could try any of the following thoughts to challenge their anxiety:

- No one has vomited all school year; chances are that it probably won't happen today either.
- If someone does get sick, I can quickly move away. I will be fine.

- The school nurse will be around to help my sick classmate.
- Normally, if someone vomits in class, the others don't get sick. I know I can stay healthy too.
- So what if someone vomit? We all get sick sometimes. It will be okay.

16. Journal your child's anxiety symptoms and responses to fears. It is wonderful encouragement for a child to see documented improvement over time especially when their perception is negative.

17. When out of your care, make sure that there is a responsible person to support your child. Be sure to communicate your child's plan to this person and have your child practice it with him or her. Most commonly, it will be a teacher or a babysitter. Having a consistent approach in all areas of your child's life will bring peace and more control to their functioning.

18. Encourage your child to participate in activities they enjoy. Despite having phobia symptoms, your child can still enjoy life. Since phobias are very specific in nature, these can commonly be set aside to engage in activities where the phobic trigger(s) are not present. Having fun is important.

19. Make sure that your child gets enough sleep. A tired person has a harder time managing anxious feelings. Symptoms are also more likely to become exaggerated when sleep is lacking.

20. Visit behaviorcorner.com for more information and contact options for getting additional guidance from a professional therapist.

ADHD: Attention,Impulsivity, and Hyperactivity

Introduction

Children who have attention deficit/hyperactivity disorder (ADHD) will engage in the same behaviors over and over—even if the consequences are negative. These children need very *clear*, *consistent*, and *predictable* limits. They have a hard time with warnings and unclear consequences. The same is true for those children who remain undiagnosed yet regularly display short attention spans, impulsive behavior, and/or hyperactive symptoms.

Children who have difficulties in this area characteristically have poorer grades in school, fewer positive peer relationships, have lower self-esteem, and have more trouble with those in authority as rules and directions are not easily followed.

Sadly, I have seen these resulting characteristics firsthand in numerous children. These are good children who want to please others, want to be liked by their peers, and who want to get good grades. However, several factors exist for these children that may not for their peers.

To begin with, the brains of children with ADHD or like symptoms are wired differently than other children who do not suffer from attentional, impulsivity, and/or hyperactive symptoms. Environmental factors also contribute to the likelihood of experiencing difficulty in this area. Those who come from chaotic homes, have inconsistent parents, those who are abused or neglected, or have any other ongoing stressors are at a much higher risk for attentional, impulsive, and hyperactive concerns.

The wonderful part in all of these finding is that there are ways to treat and reverse the effects of ADHD symptoms. Children with attentional and/or hyperactive-impulsive difficulties are more likely to respond to consequences that are consistent, positive, and rewarding.

Even more important, you can make significant changes to your children's environment as the first step in managing these childhood difficulties. It will take dedication and patience, but I know you can do it. Keep reading…

Formal Diagnosis

According to the American Psychiatry Association, a diagnosis of attention deficit/hyperactivity disorder could take one of three forms:

1. *Combined presentation* (both inattention and hyperactivity-impulsivity is seen)

    - Six or more of the inattentive symptoms plus six or more of the hyperactive-impulsive symptoms (see below bullets) must exist for at least six months, be developmentally inappropriate for the age of the child, and negatively impact their day-to-day functioning.

Common Co-Existing Conditions

- Oppositional defiant disorder
- Tic disorder
- Conduct disorder
- Anxiety
- Depression
- Substance use
- Specific learning disorder
- Autism spectrum disorder

2. *Predominantly inattentive presentation*

    - Often fails to give close attention to details or makes careless mistakes in schoolwork, work, or other activities
    - Often has difficulty sustaining attention in tasks or play activities
    - Often does not listen when spoken to directly

- Often does not follow through on instructions and fails to finish school work, chores, or duties in the workplace (not due to oppositional behaviors or failure to understand instructions)
- Often has difficulty organizing tasks and activities
- Often avoids, dislikes, or is reluctant to engage in tasks that require sustained mental effort (such as schoolwork or homework)
- Often loses things necessary for tasks or activities. (toys, school assignments, pencils, books, or tools)
- Is often easily distracted by unimportant stimuli
- Is often forgetful in daily activities

Six or more of these criteria and symptoms must exist for at least six months, be developmentally inappropriate for the age of the child, and negatively impact their day-to-day functioning.

Note: If defiance, lack of understanding, or hostility are the only causes for symptom presentation, a diagnosis of ADHD is *not* appropriate.

3. *Predominantly hyperactive/impulsive presentation*

- Often fidgets with or taps hands or feet or squirms in seat
- Often leaves their seat in the classroom or in other situations in which remaining seated is expected
- Often runs around or climbs excessively in situations in which it is inappropriate (in older children this symptom may be the child expressing that they feel restless)
- Often has difficulty playing or engaging in leisure activities quietly
- Is often "on the go" or often acts as if "driven by a motor"
- Often talks excessively

- Often blurts out answers before questions have been completed
- Often has difficulty waiting for a turn
- Often interrupts or intrudes on others (interrupts conversations or games, takes things without asking)

Six or more of these criteria and symptoms must exist for at least six months, be developmentally inappropriate for the age of the child, and negatively impact their day-to-day functioning.

Note: If defiance, lack of understanding, or hostility are the only causes for symptom presentation, a diagnosis of ADHD is *not* appropriate.

Additional criteria that will be considered as an evaluation for ADHD takes place are

- several symptoms of inattentive or hyperactive-impulsive that existed before the child turned twelve years old;
- several symptoms of inattentive or hyperactive-impulsive behaviors that are currently being seen in two or more settings such as home, school, daycare, family members' homes, in the community, etc.;
- symptoms that negatively impact the child's daily social, academic, or occupational functioning; and
- symptoms that are not better explained by another disorder.

It is important to consider some of the possible factors that may result in the life of a child with attentional and/or hyperactive-impulsive difficulties. Research shows that these children struggle academically in school, have more peer conflicts than others, struggle to maintain positive relationships with adults and peers, and have an increased risk of developing other mental disorders into adulthood.

Treatment for your child is essential!

Counselor's Corner

A few words on treatment

Over the years, I have worked with and seen countless children who display symptoms of ADHD. Some of these kids were officially diagnosed while others were not.

Scenario A: Those children who received their diagnosis, had parents willing to make changes, began medical treatment, and received regular counseling, made the greatest gains in life. They began to listen better at home, they improved their grades in school, followed more rules in various settings, and got along with others with much less conflict. It was beautiful to see such wonderful success!

Scenario B: For those children who did not have parents willing to investigate the possibility that their child was suffering from ADHD experienced unfortunate hardships in many areas of functioning. These were the kids who had the most difficulty at home and at school. They received many more negative consequences and their parents got many more negative phone calls from school and community leaders.

Scenario A or scenario B? My vote is for scenario A. It sounds just like what your child needs to feel good about themselves and what you need to raise a successful and productive person.

Note: A diagnosis of ADHD doesn't necessarily mean that your child will be given medication – that is your choice as the parent. However, there are many interventions and counseling options to address the symptoms. The more you know, the more you can do for your family – that empowers you!

Interventions

Special note: Appendix A contains plans that can help to motivate your child to increase their ability to focus. These plans are also mentioned in the following interventions.

1. Consult with your child's doctor about your concerns. Get a plan in place to have your child evaluated. Ask for referrals for a mental health professional and work together to get a thorough treatment plan in place. When a child's parents, medical team, and mental health team work together, great things can happen.

2. Visit the Counselor's Corner at behaviorcorner.com to arrange for online counseling for you and your child.

3. Use eye contact when you are speaking. For a young child, get down on their level so that you are not talking down to them. Eye contact assures that you have their attention.

4. Use positive praise and reinforcers (hugs, high fives, a sticker) to constantly let your child know how proud you are of their appropriate actions, no matter how small. Using positive reinforcement encourages your child to continue showing desirable behaviors.

5. Encouragement and praise must be used even if your child's success or efforts are small. Reinforcing these positive steps will only help them to increase.

6. Give your child advanced notice about the plans for the day along with any changes to the schedule when possible.

7. Keep your verbal requests simple and clear. Many children with ADHD can only effectively manage one-step directions. Too many words make your message hard to understand.

8. Ensure your child has complete understanding of your requests and expectations. Do this by role-playing or physically showing them what you are expecting.

9. Leave notes that praise the positive characteristics and efforts of your child.

10. Use a timer to challenge your child to perform a request in "record time." Celebrate when the task is completed.

11. Give an advance warning before the end or beginning of an activity. For example, you can say, "You have five minutes left to play before clean up begins," or "We will be leaving for the store in two minutes."

12. Use signals or sounds to help transition your child from one task to the next. Use a timer, a bell, or any other item that signals the ending of one task and the beginning of another.

13. Give your child a transition object (a stuffed animal, a favorite toy, a sign that says "on to something new") to

take from activity to activity. This helps to make ending one task and starting a new one more enjoyable.

14. When children are diagnosed with ADHD, research has found that the use of behavior modification programs along with the use of medication results in positive changes in behavior.

When creating a behavior modification plan, work with your children to establish no more than three reasonable goals or expectations that focus on their specific ADHD behaviors. Examples of how to meet the expectations should be listed along with reward options. See appendix A for an example.

The following are key foundations to a successful behavior plan:

- Provide consistent rules, structure, and boundaries.
- Include your children in creating the goals and take their opinions seriously. Help them to understand why the goals are important.
- State the goals in a simple and positive way (e.g. "Show respect to others" or "Do what you are told").
- Demonstrate and practice with your children on how to perform the goals.

Counselor's Corner

How do you set a goal with your child?
A reasonable to goal for your child should take into consideration:

- Their developmental abilities
- Their desire to have the goal
- Their motivation to meet the goal
- The availability of consistent support to help them succeed.

Without these core elements, the behavior plan will likely fail to improve your child's behavior. Worse, your child will feel unsuccessful.

- Earning privileges are a large part of a successful plan. Work together to identify the privileges you will both be happy with. Have fun with this. Your kids will!
- Include some "gimmie" goals in the plan in addition to the three original goals. These are expectations that your child can easily achieve, which results in increased success and motivation to do well in other areas of the plan too.
- Include all individuals in your home. Healthy competition can be created between siblings participating in the plan. In addition, consistency being shown by all adults will prove to be a wonderful example to your children.
- Adults in the home must follow the rules and uphold the expectations too. Children look to adults as role models.
- Monitor and discuss your children's behaviors and progress toward the behavioral goals. Depending on the age of your children, this can be done on a daily or weekly basis.
- Behavior modification programs become even more successful when you and your children's school work together. Create a daily communication tool to uphold consistent expectations.

15. Always provide for frequent positive reinforcement. Even when a long-term goal is established, it is important to recognize and reward progress. This could include earning stickers, tokens, points or anything else that is used toward meeting the larger goal. See appendix A for an example.

16. Use colorful tracking charts to show your child the progress being made toward their goals. This can be a powerful motivator along with providing your child with personal competition to make even more progress in the days

ahead. This intervention is most easily done with a piece of graph paper and crayons to create daily bar graphs.

17. Ask your child to repeat what you said in their own words. This is a great way to check for understanding and to make sure your child has truly heard what you told them.

18. Do not give several warnings and do not give lectures. These teach your child that they can gain your attention (although negative) by misbehaving.

Counselor's Corner

Easy but takes dedication

Believe me when I say that avoiding giving several warning and lectures is hard to do. It sounds easy enough; but when it comes down to it, it is less disruptive to give more than one warning versus taking time away from what you are doing to issue a consequence.
Try to not fall into this trap. The result will be frustration, deteriorating relationships, and a guarantee of more undesirable behavior in the future. ICK!

19. Set up a daily communication plan between school or daycare providers. This allows your child to know that you and their caregivers are striving toward the same goals.

20. Once a consequence is served, be sure to problem-solve with your child in order to plan for improved behavior in the future.

21. Use planned ignoring if your child is misbehaving in an attempt to get your attention. They will learn that they will receive your attention when they make better decisions.

    The exception to this strategy is if your child is hurting himself or others. You must intervene if this is the case. Reflect with your child on the reasons behind your planned ignoring so they can understand that misbehavior does not payoff.

22. Use nonverbal directives when possible, such as sign language or pointing to the rules as a reminder. Many children become unaffected by verbal requests. Eventually, it sounds like "blah, blah, blah." Nonverbal communication sends a different type of message that can be even more effective.

23. Give your child choices. A common choice should include removing themselves from the situation until they are able to return showing appropriate behavior.

Counselor's Corner

Choices are powerful

Choices give power to your children and to yourself! As a parenting rule of thumb, giving your children choices whenever possible is wonderful. Making choices encourages independence, allows your children to feel as though they have a say as an important member of their household, and conveys respect.

From a behavioral perspective, giving your children choices that include positive decisions increases the likelihood that misbehavior will stop when they see that they still hold some power.

Consider these examples:

"Running is not allowed right not. You have a choice, you can walk with us or ride in the wagon"

"Talking in a rude tone is not ok. You have a choice, you can talk to me by using a kind tone and manners or you can decide to end this conversation for now."

In both of these situations, a parent is trying to stop misbehavior. Instead of just handing over a consequence, the examples allow for a great opportunity for the child to learn from their mistake and to make a more positive choice. Awesome!

24. Include your child in activities that are interesting to them. Their interest level will be high while negative behaviors will be low.

25. When using strategies to correct behavior, record your child's progress so you can easily determine which strategies are most effective. You will also be able to figure out what changes may need to be made.

26. Behavior change takes time. Be patient, flexible, understanding, and supportive.

27. Always be consistent when upholding expectations and when giving positive and negative consequences. This will be very powerful in maintaining and increasing positive change in your child.

28. In the moment, teach your child to consider the consequences of their actions. If the consequences are not favorable, they should think about what choice to make instead.

29. When doing homework, put a cardboard or paper frame around only one problem at a time to help your child focus. You can also try drawing a line under work already done. As an alternative, try folding the paper so fewer questions are seen at one time.

30. Provide your child with a quiet and nondistracting area to complete homework. It is also helpful to face your child toward a wall or to place dividers around them so as to eliminate visual distractions.

31. Give your child a seat cushion or an exercise ball to sit on while doing homework or during other times when sitting for lengthy periods of time is necessary. These things allow for movement while sitting in one place.

32. When attending a function where your child must sit, allow them to have handheld objects to keep them busy working with the chosen item. Some ideas include pipe cleaners, Wikki Stix, Rubik's Cube, handheld video games, and clay.

33. Provide your child with daily exercise. This should be performed for at least thirty minutes per day. Exercise gives the brain a natural boost of chemicals that can assist your child in better decision-making and coping.

34. If needed, request that your child's school or daycare incorporate exercise during each day for twenty to thirty minutes. This should be in addition to what you are doing at home. This is because children thrive when exposed physical activity, especially when expected to sit for long

periods during school hours. Many schools are already providing this additional exercise, so making sure that it is in place for your child should be easy.

35. Use close proximity or gently touch your child on the shoulder, back, or head to physically remind them that you are near and are expecting them to make better choices. Your nonverbal presence can be very effective.

36. Talk to your child frequently about what they are doing. When doing this, use details and speak about what your child is specifically doing (e.g. "I see that you are treating your toys very nicely. I like how you arranged them neatly in the toy basket"). Statements like these give your child positive attention, teaches right from wrong, and shows that you love them by taking time out of your day to notice them for positive actions.

37. Create schedules for your child to follow each day. Self-esteem rises when your child finds independent success through the use of a personal schedule.
Tip: Next to each task on the schedule, leave a box or blank line for your child to check off as each one is completed. This is critical in making sure your child doesn't become confused or overwhelmed.

38. When tasks involve multiple steps, write down each step (or use pictures) to keep your child independently on the right track.

39. Show your child how to complete a task, have them repeat how to do it, and then practice it as needed.

40. Allow your child to chew gum to decrease amounts of excessive talking.

41. Set up a secret signal with your child that you use to remind them of expected behavior. Examples include the time-out signal, touching your nose, or saying a word or phrase.

42. Give you child reasons why listening to you, attending to tasks, and completing activities are important. When chil-

dren (and adults) know the reason behind doing something, they are more apt to comply. Hint: "Because I said so" is not a reason!

43. Prior to an event, ensure that your child understands the expectations.

44. The leading authority on ADHD is the Children and Adults with Attention-Deficit/Hyperactivity Disorder (CHADD). Additional information on this organization can be found at www.chadd.org/

45. Visit behaviorcorner.com for more information and contact options for getting additional guidance from a professional therapist.

Autism Spectrum Disorder

Introduction

Autism spectrum disorder (ASD) is a disorder used to describe individuals who display autistic-like characteristics as described below. As with any diagnosis, each person presents with unique symptoms. The same is true with ASD. The severity of these symptoms varies from person to person. Different levels of support will be needed based on your child's level of ASD severity and personal need. For the purpose of this reference tool, I have included an overview of behaviors commonly found in ASD along with possible interventions to use with your child. Due to the wide range of functioning that children display, it is important for you to personally select the interventions that make the most sense for your child and family. After all, you know your child best, and early intervention is key.

Those diagnosed with ASD are found to display some or all of the following characteristics. These symptoms will range from mild to severe depending on your child's unique needs.

- Lack of social communication
- Difficulty understanding nonverbal communication
- Difficulty forming and maintaining peer relationships
- Using self-stimulating behaviors such as finger wiggling, hand flapping, and rocking
- Hurting oneself
- Displaying repetitive and highly focused behaviors
- Displaying aggression toward objects and people
- Having a hard time understanding and responding to environmental stimulation

- Must have a daily routine with plenty of preventative steps built into the day in order to manage conflicts (internal or external) and/or to manage unexpected changes to their routine
- Obsessions with objects or activities in which looking at pictures, talking, or drawing may consume the majority of their focus
- Does not see the "gray areas" in situations and inflexible to alternate ways of thinking

Formal Diagnosis

According to the American Psychiatric Association, autism spectrum disorder is described as thus:

- Continuous deficits in social communication and social interaction in many different situations. Such as:

  o Deficits in social and emotional exchange (ranging from no back-and-forth conversations; little to no interest in sharing emotions, interests, or affect; and failure to initiate or respond to social interactions)

  o Deficits in nonverbal communication used for social interaction (ranging from a poor ability to pair verbal and nonverbal communication, abnormal eye contact and body language, difficulty understanding and using gestures, to a total lack of facial expressions and nonverbal communication)

Common Co-Existing Conditions

- Attention-deficit/hyperactivity disorder
- Pica
- Medical conditions
- Intellectual disabilities
- Structural language disorder
- Learning disabilities
- Anxiety disorders
- Sensory processing deficits

- Deficits in developing, maintaining, and understanding relationships (ranging from difficulties in adjusting behavior to meet situations, difficulties in sharing imaginative play or in making new friends, to no interest in peers)

- Limited and repetitive patterns of behaviors, interests, or activities as demonstrated by at least two of the following:

  - Repetitive and frequent non-goal orientated motor movements, use of objects (lining toys up in a specific way), or speech (repeating words or phrases)

  - Inflexible to things that are different. Insistence on routines, or ritualized patterns of verbal or nonverbal behavior (same food every day, greetings, transition routines)

  - Highly limited and fixated interests that are abnormal in intensity or focus

  - Over or underreactive to sensory stimuli or has an unusual interest in sensory features of the environment (sounds, texture, temperature, smells, lights, movement)

  - Autism spectrum disorder symptoms must have been present during early development (full symptoms may not show themselves until social demands increase)

  - Symptoms cause significant impairment in daily life and functioning

  - Symptoms are not better explained by intellectual disability or global developmental delay

Raising a child with ASD is challenging. Thankfully there are many helpful resources available to you. The interventions listed below will get you started. However, to gain the most help for your child and family visit, www.autismspeaks.org to get linked up with community supports.

Early intervention is key!

Interventions

1. Consult with a doctor or therapist experienced in working with children with autism spectrum disorder to help you identify a plan that will meet your child's unique needs. A child specific plan should include

   - the child's strengths and weaknesses;
   - the child's likes and dislikes;
   - the child's support system;
   - several strategies to be implemented and when to use them;
   - successful strategies used in the past or present that give emotional and educational support;
   - identified triggers or stressors;
   - unique ways in which the child communicates their needs and wants; and
   - the places, activities, and people who bring the best out of your child along with where and with whom your child struggles the most.

2. Visit the Counselor's Corner at behaviorcorner.com to arrange for online counseling for you and your child.
3. Get your child treatment as soon as possible. Even if a diagnosis is not official, autism spectrum disorder symptoms need to be treated immediately. The sooner a child receives treatment to address delays, the better the outcome.
4. Ask questions and join a support group. Gaining knowledge and participating in the treatment plan of your child will further promote positive results. Having the facts will help you to make informed decisions.

5. Gather the team working with your child. Teachers, therapists, doctors, caregivers, family members, and so on need to be able to communicate with you and with each other. This communication helps treatment become more effective because everyone can use the same strategies in all settings. Doing so results in increased coping and learning for your child.

6. Be proactive. You know your child best. Use this to your benefit as you identify stressors and triggers that upset your child. Depending on the situation and on your child's level of functioning, you can problem-solve these situations or work to avoid them.

7. Visit www.thegraycenter.org to learn about the extremely useful strategy called social stories. Social stories help children understand social skills and help to promote flexibility and problem-solving by writing situation specific stories with your child as the main character.

8. Ensure that there is a plan in place for your child while away from home. Typically this will mean an Individualized Education Plan (IEP) or a behavior plan at school and daycare. Proactive and positive strategies from therapy and home should be included on the plan and updated frequently. Progress reports should be sent to you regularly as well.

9. When communicating with your child, use clear visuals such as sign language, gestures, pictures, symbols, written words, or art alongside your spoken word. For example, if you are telling your child to sit down, use the sign language visual at the same time.

10. Provide consistent routines. Each day should be mapped out so that your child can expect the next task or activity. It is helpful to keep a visual schedule where activities that have been completed can be flipped upside down or physically taken off of the schedule. Using a system with Velcro to attach and remove tasks works well here.

11. Keep consistent rules to prevent your child from becoming overwhelmed and frustrated from mixed messages as to what is acceptable and what isn't.

12. Provide your child with a picture of the next activity prior to telling them to switch tasks. For example, if your child is using the computer and you need to get to the grocery store, tell them that they have five minutes left on the computer and then you will be going shopping. Show a picture of the grocery that you are going to. Of course, the trip to the grocery store should have been on the schedule from the start of the day, which will help to make this transition much smoother.

13. Leave home prepared. Children with autism spectrum disorder tend to be overly sensitive to stimuli such as sounds, smells, and brightness. Knowing this about your child will help you to plan your daily errands. Even when you try to avoid these things, it is a good idea to bring along known calming items and activities to help your child cope if they become overwhelmed.

14. Create a chore system so your child will know exactly what needs to be done, when to start, how to know they are finished, and what happens when the work is complete.

15. Give plenty of rewards. Children with autism spectrum disorder respond well to positive incentives. Go out of your way to praise them for good decisions and tell them ahead of time what they can earn for specific behaviors. You may need to remind your child frequently of the behaviors that will result in a reward. Follow through on the praise and reward every time to promote increased learning.

16. Give your child a quiet place to complete homework or to relax with minimal to no distractions.

17. Create a calming place for your child to spend time when feeling overstimulated or upset. Marking this place with pictures, decorating a large box or divider, or using a color-coded system are a few examples of effective ways to iden-

tify this calming area. Your child may go to this place on their own or may need your assistance the first few times until they comprehend what the space is for.

In the calming place, post pictures of calming skills (deep breathing, pictures of a calming place, counting, etc.) along with the calming tools available to your child such as a weighted blanket or vest, ball, clay, toys, etc.

18. Pay close attention to the ways in which your child is communicating with you. All children have their own way of acting when they need something, want something, or are upset. Regardless of a child's speech and language abilities, they communicate if we are willing to listen.

19. Get them to bed. Do your best to make sure your child is getting enough sleep at night. Most school-aged children need at least ten hours of sleep per night.

20. Patience, patience, patience. No doubt, there is a lot of preparation that goes into scheduling, routines, visuals, and so on. It can be frustrating at times to have to preplan every move of your day ahead of time. However, planning and meeting your child's individual needs helps your child learn lifelong skills to be successful. This will pay off if you are consistent. Learning will happen slowly, but remember that your child has a lifetime to learn. Lean on your support group to help you prepare and to feel proud of how you are meeting your child's needs.

Whether a parent of a child who has an autism spectrum disorder or not, the goal of all parents is to raise children using all the tools necessary for them to grow into the most successful person possible. Embrace this challenge and give it all you've got. You are not alone.

21. Unconditional love, acceptance, and support are huge pieces in helping your child become the best that they can be. Be thankful for your child just the way they are and accept them as a valuable human being.

22. Participate in activities that your child finds fun and interesting. Spend time together and do things that your child wants to do. This does wonders for bonding and allows them to enjoy childhood.

23. Take care of yourself. In order to take care of your family, you need to be healthy and strong. Caring for a child with autism spectrum disorder takes a lot of dedication. Don't forget about your own needs during this process.
Leaving your child with a trusted caregiver for a short time, getting enough exercise, eating healthy, doing some online shopping, seeing a counselor, going to a marriage camp, or doing anything else to strengthen your being and your family will benefit you all.

24. Rely on your support system. Learning that your child has autism spectrum disorder is hard to handle. There are many questions, worries, and frustrations that go along with this parenting venture. Family, friends, and professionals are key people that will help to support you.

25. Visit behaviorcorner.com for more information and contact options for getting additional guidance from a professional therapist.

Bipolar Disorder

Introduction

Bipolar is a disorder that is diagnosed by a mental health and/or medical professional. It is a severe diagnosis that must be taken seriously. It is wise to ensure that your child has received a thorough evaluation before accepting a diagnosis of bipolarity. The doctor or mental health professional should be experienced in diagnosing and treating bipolar disorder. This is especially true because there are several theories of thought on how bipolar presents in children. In addition, there are overlapping symptoms and conditions that need to be closely considered to reach an accurate diagnosis of mental disorder(s).

Formal Diagnosis

According to the American Psychiatric Association, the seven bipolar and related disorders are as follows:

1. bipolar I disorder
2. bipolar II disorder
3. cyclothymic disorder
4. substance/medication-induced bipolar and related disorder
5. bipolar and related disorder due to another medical condition
6. other specified bipolar and related disorder
7. unspecified bipolar and related disorder

Common Co-Existing Conditions

- Attention-deficit/hyperactivity disorder
- Conduct disorder
- Oppositional defiant disorder
- Anxiety disorders
- Substance use
- Suicide risk
- Medical conditions
- Eating disorder
- Sleep disorders

Within these seven diagnoses, there are several factors to consider. Each one has many different criteria sets in order to identify if a person truly suffers from a bipolar disorder. Although this chapter will start to give you a sense of what bipolar diagnoses are about, it is beyond the scope of this book to go into the many layers that make up an individual bipolar diagnosis.

Again, I strongly encourage you to contact a professional who is well versed in identifying the symptoms of bipolar in children. They will know how to treat it and can effectively guide you in home based interventions.

Each bipolar diagnosis addresses several factors focused on manic episodes (must last at least one week), hypomanic episodes (must last at least four days), major depressive episodes (must last at least two weeks), manic and hypomanic symptoms, and/or depressive symptoms.

Keep in mind that bipolar symptoms will not present as the same in each child. Just as we are all unique individuals, bipolar symptoms are shown in personal ways. Special consideration must be given and each child must be evaluated as per their own functioning and history in order to make an accurate diagnosis.

> Bipolarity is complicated and is a very serious disorder. Contact a medical or mental health professional who specializes in bipolar. Ask your child's doctor for referrals.

Symptoms of a bipolar diagnosis in children may include

- severe separation anxiety;
- a hard time dealing with transitions and new situations;
- temper tantrums;
- worsening disruptive behavior, extreme moodiness;
- sleep problems;
- aggressive episodes followed by grief and remorse;
- declining academic progress;
- increased impulsivity;

- decreased concentration and ability to handle frustration;
- hyperactive;
- hypersexual;
- extreme emotional swings from happiness to anger;
- bedwetting and daytime accidents beyond the normal age; and
- times of consistent sleep and slow thinking and then times of extreme energy.

There are three main features of bipolar: manic, hypomanic, and depressive. Cycling between these features occurs rapidly in children diagnosed with bipolarity. These characteristics may last anywhere from a few hours to a few days.

Manic and hypomanic characteristics may include

- abnormal and repeated joyfulness, silliness, and goofiness;
- unusual happiness;
- optimistic moods;
- explosive;
- exaggerated sense of self-confidence;
- inappropriate sexual fixations that were previously nonexistent;
- decreased need for sleep;
- sense of self-importance and superiority over others;
- excessive irritability;
- distractibility;
- aggression;
- hyperactivity;
- speaking at a rapid, loud and constant pace;
- racing thoughts;

Counselor's Corner

Manic vs. hypomanic. What's the difference?

Manic	Hypomanic
Abnormal and continuous elevated, expansive, or irritable mood and abnormally and continuously increased goal-directed activity or energy	Abnormal and continuous elevated, expansive, or irritable mood and abnormally and continuous increased activity or energy
Lasts at least 1 week for most of each day and for nearly every day during the episode	Lasts for at least 4 days for most of each day and for nearly every day during the episode
Can last for any duration of time if hospitalization is necessary	No hospitalization
Episodes are severe enough to cause significant impairment in daily functioning or to result in hospitalization	Episodes are not severe enough to cause significant impairment on daily functioning to result in hospitalization
Possible psychotic features	No psychotic features
Dangerous or high consequence behaviors	Behaviors are seen as more erratic and impulsive than dangerous
Is not due to another medical condition or a result of substance use	Is not due to the effects of a substance

- jumping from one topic to the next;
- missing steps in logical thinking;
- extreme impulsiveness and distractibility;
- poor judgment;
- laughing uncontrollably;
- reckless and perhaps dangerous behavior;
- changes in dress to wild and unusual;
- increases in goal-directed activity;
- takes on many tasks at the same time;
- makes unrealistic plans for project completions;
- may have auditory or visual hallucinations; and
- engages excessively in pleasurable activities that have a high risk for negative consequences.

> The best way to remember the difference between manic and hypomanic symptoms is to think of hypomania as a less intense form of mania.

Depressive characteristics may include

- sadness doesn't go away,
- feeling empty inside,
- frequent crying for a variety of reasons,
- change in appetite that results in either weight loss or weight gain,
- failure to make adequate weight gain,
- change in sleeping pattern,
- lack of energy,
- fatigue,
- irritable mood,
- agitation,
- anger,
- anxiety,
- tearfulness,
- having a negative outlook on life,
- feelings of guilt and worthlessness,

- inability to concentrate or make decisions,
- loss of pleasure in usual things,
- withdrawal from relationships,
- no interest in school or work,
- aches and pains that do not have a medical cause, and
- recurring thoughts of death or suicide.

A child who has a true bipolar disorder will benefit from medications, mental health therapy, and a supportive and consistent environment at home.

Interventions

1. If your child is in crisis, call 1-800-273-8255 to speak to a trained counselor. This is a national support hotline.
2. Take many precautions to keep your child and family safe. Due to the swing in manic to depressive symptoms, it is your duty to ensure that proper safety measures are taken and maintained. A few examples include learning how to safely restrain your child if needed, removing any weapons from the home, staying tuned to nonverbal and negative body language, addressing any suicidal thoughts, and looking for signs of drug or alcohol use.
3. In order to be a positive and supportive family member, you must deal with your own feelings about your child having bipolar disorder. Gain knowledge and support from others to help your manage your feelings and level of acceptance.

    None of this is your fault or your child's fault. Your child needs you. You can be their greatest asset in navigating through this diagnosis.
4. Stay in close contact with your child's pediatrician and with a mental health provider. These two support professionals will be your greatest assets in your quest to help your child.

5. Arrange individual counseling for your child. You child will have the opportunity to learn and practice coping skills and social skills as well as gain awareness to their environment. Improved self-esteem, medication compliance, and overall improved functioning in daily activities are further benefits to counseling.

6. Arrange for those living in your household to attend family counseling. Family counseling can assist everyone in learning about bipolar. It can also help to educate you on positive parenting skills, strategies to use, and coping skills.

7. Give permission for providers, teachers, and any other professional working with your child to communicate with one another. With your consent, providers can share ideas and keep each other updated. Request that you get regular updates as well.

8. Provide daily structure, routine, and consistency. Your child will be able to handle daily expectations better when they know what to anticipate.

9. When speaking about medications that are used to treat bipolarity, keep in mind that several medications may be needed to effectively treat this disorder. Trial and error in discovering what works best for your child is to be expected. Be patient with this progress.

10. Provide a safe and quiet area that your child can use as a time-away spot. This could be a under a table covered with a blanket or in a big box with holes. Be creative and ask for your child's input into what they feel would comfort them the most.

11. Choose your battles carefully. There are some things that truly do not need to be addressed. Consider the end result of addressing an issue versus just letting it go. Use your judgment wisely.

12. When having your child evaluated for bipolar disorder, consider the symptoms that your child is displaying *and*

genetics that may put your child at greater risk for bipolar disorder. When both parents have bipolar disorder, there is a 50 percent plus chance that the child will also have bipolar disorder. When one parent carries the bipolar gene, there is up to a 30 percent chance that offspring will develop bipolar disorder

13. Positives work better than negatives so phrase your instructions and consequences in a positive manner whenever possible. For example, "I am so proud of the way you went to the time-away area today. You went there without yelling and returned willing to talk. Let's have that talk now to problem-solve the situation so that you may not have to go to time-out in the future"

14. Enforce your household expectations and consequences with consistency, compassion, and fairness.

15. Establish a behavior modification program where your child earns privileges instead of losing them. A great way to do this is to reward positive behavior with points or tokens. These tokens/points can be turned in for agreed upon privileges. Here are a few points of special note:

    • When a negative consequence needs to be given, the points/tokens are off-limits and cannot be used until your child has served the consequence.
    • Never take away points or tokens that are already earned.
    • This type of behavior system allows for your child to earn privileges and to avoid feeling defeated by losing privileges previously earned.

16. Help your child learn how to control their actions by teaching them to identify their triggers and options for coping.

17. Monitor your child's sensitivity to light and sound. Either of these could be a trigger to a mood change that may not be easily identified.

18. Keep in contact with your child's teacher regarding school behavior, needs, and use of strategies. If you feel a formal plan is needed to help your child succeed in school, contact the building principal and the director of special education.

19. Use social stories to teach coping skills, problem-solving skills, and to help your child understand the connection between behavior and consequences. For more information on this, visit: www.thegraycenter.org

20. Document your child's moods. List the time of day, duration of moods, and what occurred immediately prior to mood shifts. Reflecting back upon this data can be very helpful for outside professionals working with your family.

    It can also be beneficial for you to identify what may be triggers for your child and to decide what you can preventatively put into place to lessen the likelihood of them experiencing difficulty in the future.

21. Never ignore statements that your child says about suicide, harming himself, or harming others. Take these statements seriously and get your child help.

22. Don't overreact when your child displays extreme symptoms.

23. Try your best to have a calm state of mind. This will help you to think more clearly and will help to calm your child as well.

24. Recognize your child's accomplishments and be positive whenever possible.

Defiance and Disruptive Disorders

Introduction

Defiance is displayed when children refuse to follow rules and the directions of those in authority. This is typically seen with parents, teachers, and other caregivers. Defiant children use inappropriate behaviors such as being rude, refusing to do what they are told, and causing disruptions. Parents and teachers are normally very frustrated with these children and wish that they could find a way to help increase compliance.

All behavior has purpose. What is your child's behavior telling you?

Disruptive disorders that are listed in this section include oppositional defiant disorder (ODD) and conduct disorder (CD).

Oppositional defiant disorder may be diagnosed when a child displays a regular pattern of defiance, disobedience, and hostility toward authority figures.

Conduct disorder may be diagnosed when a repetitive and continuous pattern of behavior violates the basic rights of others or of major age-appropriate societal norms or rules.

Regardless of a disorder being identified, the majority of defiant children lack positive experiences in their life and may have parents who are authoritarian in nature. This type of parenting style reinforces punishment rather than discipline (teaching) and does not take into consideration the feelings, needs, or wants of the child. It is a "do as I say, no matter what" approach to raising kids. Needless to say,

Counselor's Corner

Don't get me wrong....

There are certainly times where your kids need to obey with no questions asked. However, the majority of the directions and decisions must consider your child's feelings and desires. Follow this advice and you will raise a respectful, well-rounded person who has empathy for others.

this is unhealthy. As a result, we see these children displaying defiance and longing for control over their lives. This may result in negative behaviors in an effort to obtain this control.

Over time, the tension between child and parent worsens as the child's response to punishment results in the learning of how to use defiance to get their needs met.

Another scenario where we see this strong desire for control is when children's lives are chaotic and violent.

Lack of routines, having several caregivers, lack of supervision, lack of a loving and nurturing home, marital problems between parents, financial stress, multiple moves, and lack of positive consistency can all result in children using defiant behavior and seeking control.

Defiant behavior may lead to a diagnosis of a disruptive disorder. Research has shown that there has been a significant rise in disruptive disorder cases that are directly related to poor home environments.

Make sure your home doesn't fall into that trap. Take these steps to begin creating a positive home environment:

- Reduce the amount of time your child spends watching television and playing video games.
- Eliminate your child's exposure to violence in your home, which includes what is seen on television and in video games.
- Have clear and consistent expectations in your home. Consequences need to be fully understood and consistent as well.
- Make sure your child gets adequate sleep and exercise and that he participates in extracurricular activities
- Show daily love and acceptance to your child.
- Spend time with your child each day.

As the parent, you have control over these situations and can make change a reality for the benefit of your family. The environment you provide for your children predicts how they will interpret the world and how they will behave in it—even as adults. Don't let your shortcomings result in a diagnosis or a behavior problem for your child. The environment you provide is your responsibility, and you have a duty to ensure that the negative factors that contribute to a disruptive disorder are nonexistent.

Older children will require intense interventions and need a longer time to begin making behavioral changes. Obtaining the support of a mental health professional and supportive services for your home will work to greatly enhance the following interventions.

Formal Diagnosis: Oppositional Defiant Disorder

According to the American Psychiatry Association, oppositional defiant disorder is identified when there is a pattern of an angry/irritable mood, augmentative/defiant behavior, or vindictiveness shown by at least four of the following:

Common Co-Existing Conditions

- Attention-deficit/hyperactivity disorder
- Anxiety
- Conduct disorder
- Depression
- Substance use
- Other disorders as adults

- Often loses temper
- Is touchy or easily annoyed
- Is often angry and resentful
- Often argues with authority figures or with adults
- Purposely defies or refuses to comply with requests from authority figures or with the rules
- Purposefully annoys others
- Blames others for personal mistakes or misbehaviors
- Has been spiteful or vindictive at least twice within the past six months

The symptoms must last at least six months and occur during interactions with at least one person who is not a sibling.

In giving this diagnosis, consideration is given to the child's age, culture, situation, frequency of behaviors, gender, developmental level, and to the impact that the behaviors have on daily functioning.

Children who suffer from oppositional defiant disorder are typically cast off by their peers. This is due to their poor social skills, difficulty with problem-solving, and aggression. When faced with a social dilemma, they are more likely to resort to physical aggression rather than using their words to find a solution. Furthermore, children with ODD rarely take responsibility for their behavior. They tend to blame others for their actions ("She made me do it").

To find the professional help that your child needs, ask their pediatrician along with the counselor or social worker at your child's school for local referrals. These individuals will be able to provide you with therapeutic and community resources.

When more than a basic behavior plan is needed, it is important to get the whole family involved with community resources such as counseling, parenting support classes, and medical consultations.

Interventions

1. Pay attention to possible causes of behavior problems. These are areas that should be dealt with immediately.

    - Low self-esteem
    - Depression
    - Chemical and brain disorders
    - Family problems
    - Problems of impulse control
    - Immaturity
    - Other physical or emotional problems

Working alongside your child's pediatrician and mental health counselor will help to address these concerns appropriately.

2. Visit the Counselor's Corner at behaviorcorner.com to arrange for online counseling for you and your child.

3. Choose your battles carefully. Try not to argue or force compliance. These two things only serve to escalate hostile interactions. Use strategies such as planned ignoring, calmly give choices, calmly giving consequences, and letting the topic go until your child is calm. At that time, be ready to discuss how to use more appropriate behaviors.

4. Attend parenting classes to learn how to manage your child's defiance, how to use positive discipline, and how to de-escalate volatile situations. The right parenting class can help you to learn how to anticipate triggers to difficult behavior, how to safely calm your child, and how to safely handle anger.

5. Discipline appropriately. This includes

   • clear and simple communication of behavioral expectations;
   • setting appropriate limits;
   • monitoring and supervising children's behavior carefully;
   • providing positive attention, rewards, and privileges for effort shown toward meeting expectation;
   • using strategies such as planned ignoring, time-outs, redirecting, and/or restricting privileges when they do not meet expectations; and
   • teaching and reinforcing appropriate behaviors and choices at every opportunity.

6. Give many more positive reinforcements for behaviors over negative corrections. Recognizing even small gains and efforts is a positive way to increase desired behaviors.

Counselor's Corner

For some children, negative attention is sought out just as much or more then positive attention. Yelling, punishing, and negatively acknowledging behaviors are all ways children receive negative attention for their behaviors. For children who crave any and all attention, these strategies only serve to reinforce their behavior.

If your child is fits this mold, planned ignoring and positive recognition of desired skills is your first step on your way to positive change.

7. Do not give in to tantrums, nagging, or aggression. This only encourages defiance to continue.

8. Be patient, consistent, and as positive as possible. Acceptable behavior happens over time and is highly influenced by parents, peers, life experiences, and interventions used by adults.

9. Attempt to identify your child's triggers to becoming defiant. Do this by asking yourself, "What happened just before the behavior occurred?" Once you have it figured out, use incentives to motivate your child to have a more productive outcome in the future. Future planning for success is part of the learning process for both of you. For more information on using incentives and how they differ from bribery, visit the "Must-Know Parenting Strategies" chapter.

10. Identify what purpose the behavior is serving. Do this by asking yourself, "What happened after the behavior occurred?" This will help you to evaluate your own behavior and environmental factors that may be reinforcing negative behaviors.

11. Do not always assume that you know why your child behaved in a certain way. Once calm, ask questions and try to get your child's opinion in order to get accurate

information. Normally, there are primary and secondary feelings and reasons for a behavior.

Children commonly will identify the surface (or secondary) feeling or blame someone/something for causing that feeling. Encourage your child to look deeper into other feelings that may also be present.

> Primary and secondary emotions
> can tell a lot about a situation.

12. Work with your child and caregivers to try to identify what increases anxiety along with what the triggers may be for negative behavior choices. Anxiety may play a role in negative behavior choices as your child struggles to process anxious feelings.

13. Use distractions and redirect your child away from an upsetting situation to avoid a disruption.

14. Ignore unwanted behavior. Ignoring works by attention *not* being given to your child. If they are getting nothing out of performing the behavior (attention from you and others), the behavior may stop. The exception to this strategy is if your child is engaging in harmful or dangerous behavior. You must intervene if that occurs.

15. Increase the rate of rewards for behavior you want.

16. Provide consistent consequences for inappropriate behavior (see the consequences chapter).

17. Focus on solutions rather than just the problem.

18. Do not bring up past problems. Focus only on the current issue and possible solutions.

19. Provide a safe, private place to allow for escape and a chance to decrease negative feelings.

20. Use a behavior plan. (See appendix A)

21. Use a behavior plan at home and at school. These should tie into each other and must be reflected upon regularly

by you, your child, the school staff, and a mental health provider (if one is working with your child or family).

22. Always give choices. These choices should be options that you and your child are comfortable with. By doing this you are encouraging them to make a positive choice while instilling a feeling of control by making their own decisions. Since control is something that is frequently sought from defiant kids, this can be a powerful strategy.

23. Use your household expectations and rules to consistently set limits and boundaries. Children crave structure and boundaries. Without consistent limits and boundaries, children do not know how to behave. Parents and children end up becoming frustrated when clear limits are not in place. Starting this today and holding firm are two of the most effective ways to teach your children to use positive behavioral choices.

24. Participate in activities that foster parent-child bonding. These include reading, shopping, wrestling, having conversations, doing crafts, showing affection, and expressing positive feelings for one another.

    Children who are raised in a supportive household, who feel that they contribute to their family's well-being, and who know that they are loved unconditionally have less of a need to be defiant. These are the children who are motivated to please their caregivers by making positive choices much of the time.

25. Provide opportunities for your child to show responsibility and reinforce them for a job a well done.

26. Give calm, clear, direct, and specific instructions.

    • Reduce your talk time; be specific, clear, and brief.
    • Give only one instruction at a time.
    • Allow at least ten seconds for your child to respond.
    • Repeat an instruction no more than once; use a negative consequence if your child is still not responding.

Do this every time! Being consistent with this one will teach your child that you mean business and the only payoff received for not following directions is an undesirable consequence.

• Give instructions while using eye contact instead of shouting through the house.

Counselor's Corner

The best thing I ever did.
After what seemed like an eternity of not taking my own advice to get my children to comply, I finally did it. What you ask? I followed the above suggestions.
And guess what??? It worked!!

27. When your child is agitated, it is critical to not overwhelm them. Feeling overwhelmed leads to further defiance and loss of trust in you as the parent to help. Here are some helpful tips for working with your child when they are upset:

• Give your child a reasonable amount of time to calm down.

• When speaking, use a calm voice. Do not speak to your child in front of others. Privacy is important. If your child continues to be agitated, give them additional calming time.

• Always be available by saying, "If you need help, let me know." Even if your child has been rude in response to your offer in the past, say it anyway.

• If your child becomes upset and is unable to complete a chore or task that you have requested, that task must be made up at a later time. This shows your child that they have responsibilities and that negative behavior responses will not relieve them of these responsibilities.

- Do not engage in a power struggle with your child and do not respond to their questions or comments while either of you are upset. These two things put your child in charge, not you.

28. Create your household rules with everyone present.

- Be willing to listen to everyone's opinion and to negotiate.
- Establish positive and negative consequences associated with each rule.
- Ensure that the rules and consequences are clearly stated.
- Post the rules and consequences as reminders and as a reference tool. This can be done by hanging them on the fridge or creating a poster.
- If you have young children, the use of pictures to remind them of the rules can be helpful.
- Uphold the rules consistently and without fail.

29. Once a plan is established, revisit your household rules at least every other week.
30. The entire family should use role-playing activities to practice the rules and expectations of your home. When full understanding of how to perform the rules is established, only then can a parent hold their children accountable for their behavior.
31. Communicate with your child's teachers to ensure that strategies being used are consistent between home and school. Having daily communication is a great way to accomplish this.
32. Experiment with using indirect reinforcement by whispering, giving a thumbs-up, leaving notes, and provid-

ing rewards without a normal verbal comment. For some children, this type of praise is accepted better than being spoken to, even for great things. Use what works best for your child.

33. Always be consistent. Plan strategies that you can implement regularly.

34. Never ever call your children "bad." It is the behavior that is dissatisfying, not the child. Be sure to tell your child that they are *not* bad. However, the choices that they made are not what you expect. We can all learn from our mistakes and make better choices in the future.

    Calmly and lovingly supporting your children through this process will show how much you love them.

35. Never use hitting or name calling as a negative consequence. If you do these things, your child is learning that these negative responses are acceptable behaviors.

36. Look at your child as a whole person. Each of us have strengths and weaknesses. Your child is no exception to this. Take some time to regularly acknowledge their strengths.

37. Promote self-esteem and confidence whenever possible. Catch your child doing good things, no matter how insignificant the accomplishment might be. This is very important, as children with behavior difficulties typically have low self-esteem.

38. For every negative consequence, try to recognize your child in four or more positive ways. These times of recognition should be specific to the positive behavior you are seeing and contain details of what is being done right.

    Research has found that praise that is behavior-specific and delivered in a positive and genuine manner is one of the most effective tools for motivating people. Praise should always be immediate, frequent, enthusiastic, descriptive, and given by using eye contact.

39. Behavior plans and strategies must be applied across all settings of your child's day and with each caregiver to be most effective.

40. Provide opportunities for your child to restate expectations. For example, ask your child to state what you just said by using their own words.

41. Encourage your child to monitor their own behavior by saying, "Tell me, what is terrific about what you are doing right now?"

42. Give consistent messages about what you expect and the positive and negative consequences associated with their chosen behavior.

43. Encourage your child to become an expert on what they need to make the best choices. Give them guidance through this process.

44. Remind them that they are in control of their own behaviors; thus, the consequences received are based on their behavior, not yours.

45. If your child takes medication, avoid connecting good behavior to medication compliance. We are still responsible for our actions with or without medication.

46. Use time-outs as one of the negative consequences you agree upon with your children. This should last one minute per each year of age of your child. Children should be given the option of volunteering for a time-out when they feel that they are losing control or have made a poor choice. Give praise if your child uses a time-out on their own.

47. Requests should be given with a firm, calm, quiet tone of voice and stated within approximately three feet of your child once eye contact has been established.

48. Use a silly voice as a distraction tool to redirect your child's focus. No negative gestures or expressions should be used.

49. Teach your child social skills. These skills need to include empathy, anger management, dealing with disappoint-

ment, communicating feelings, problem-solving, and cooperating with others.

Counselor's Corner

It is not uncommon for parents to struggle with providing social skills training to their children. The ability to do this effectively has a lot to do with the age of your child and the intensity of the defiance that your child is displaying.

Contacting local mental health providers can get you started on the right path to finding a social skills group for your child. You may also consider having your child meet individually with a mental health provider to work on social skills.

Regardless of your choice, keep in mind that your child will need social skills to navigate their way through childhood, and also as an adult. Do your child the favor of preparing them for the world by getting them help they need.

Admitting that you can't do it all on your own is perfectly acceptable. When you do, you are sending the message that your children come first and you are willing to do whatever it takes to make sure they are healthy and turn out to be productive members of society.

Appendix D provides you with teachable examples of social skills.
Take a look, have fun, find success, and smile!

50. Allow your child to release anger through exercise or by working with clay, stress balls, or any other type of material and work out his frustrations in an appropriate manner. These are wonderful ways to teach your child how to manage emotions.

51. When calm, ask your child how they would feel if their actions were to be seen in a movie or on television for all to see. Ask, "Would you feel proud?" or "What would you change?"

52. Teach your child to talk about their feelings instead of acting on them. Give them choices to use verbal words, written words, or drawings to communicate. Provide a safe place for your child to keep their written work until an established time when you two can look it over.

53. Develop a predictable daily schedule and allow your child advanced notice if there are any changes. Predictability keeps anxiety, stress, and frustrations low.

54. When speaking with your child about their behavior, remember that humans are not motivated to change behavior that isn't seen as a problem. For change to happen, you and your child have to see a need and feel a desire to make the change.

Counselor's Corner

Humans in general will not make changes or be willing to change behaviors that they feel are not a problem.

Even if your child will not discuss future plans for managing feelings or situations, rest assured that you are a sending a loving and supportive message when you offer your time to talk with them.

Keep on trying and do your best to stay consistent and supportive.

Even if it feels as though you are not getting through to your child, I guarantee you that they notice that you are trying and may one day take you up on your offer to open up.

No one says that parenting is an easy job. As a matter of fact, it is the hardest job on earth when done correctly!

Push forward my friend. Your rewards will be great.

55. When your child is doing something that could result in trouble, stop the activity and ask them what they're doing. Emphasize that your goal in this is to help keep them out of trouble.

56. Acknowledge your child's feelings and wants. Be willing to negotiate. This allows your child to feel that they have a voice as they strive for some independence.

57. When giving a first request, use the word "please" and give your child at least ten seconds of wait time. If successful, give positive reinforcement.

   If your child does not comply, a second request is started with "You need to," wait time is given, and choices are offered. Reinforcement is given if your child complies. If there is no compliance, a consequence is given. This process *must* be used consistently.

58. Say exactly what you want by keeping your requests and/ or explanations short and to the point. A good rule is to keep your communication within fifteen to twenty words. Long lectures will do no good.

59. Use phrases like "Show me..." and "Tell me about it..." This shows interest in your child and requires more than a one-word response. As a bonus, you may be able to gather information to be used to give a positive praise.

60. Make requests to your child by deferring control. For example, "The clock says it is time to go" is heard very differently than your request of "It's time to go."

61. Be empathetic as you anticipate problems by saying, "I know this might be difficult..." This will prepare your child for what comes next. With your help, they can think about some ways to problem-solve the situation even before it occurs.

62. Have fun and help your child feel good about their positive actions. Even though you may have to look hard to find them, I guarantee you that they exist. Keep looking!

63. Be a positive role model for your child by managing your emotions in a positive manner (see appendix B), learning to admit your mistakes, and making sure to follow all the expectations and rules of the home.

64. Be proactive by establishing consequences before problems occur. This allows for a greater understanding of what will happen after certain actions.

Providing your child with this information gives them a *chance* and a *choice* (two very important ways to empower your child) in making their own decisions. After all, your child is in charge of their own actions. Just be sure to implement the positive and negative consequences consistently.

65. Listen to your child before reacting. This makes them feel heard and valued. As a member of your family, they should be treated with respect just as you expect it from them.

66. Be willing to walk away before a situation escalates.

67. Discuss problems privately. When in the presence of others, defiant children feel the need to find control in the situation. They will try to exert that control especially when in the presence of others.

68. If medication is tried, it should be in conjunction with mental health therapy to gain the most favorable results. A method to gather data on the benefits and drawbacks of the medication should also be put into place.

69. Visit behaviorcorner.com for more information and contact options for getting additional guidance from a professional therapist.

Formal Diagnosis: Conduct Disorder

According to the American Psychiatry Association, conduct disorder is identified when a repetitive and continuous pattern of behavior violates the basic rights of others or of major age-appropriate societal norms or rules. This behavior is demonstrated by the following:

- Often bullies, threatens, or intimidates others
- Often initiates physical fights
- Has used a weapon that can cause serious physical harm to others
- Has been physically cruel to people
- Has been physically cruel to animals
- Has stolen while confronting a victim
- Has forced someone into sexual activity

Common Co-Existing Conditions

- Attention-deficit/hyperactivity disorder
- Oppositional defiant disorder
- Anxiety
- Depression
- Bipolar disorder
- Posttraumatic stress disorder
- Obsessive compulsive disorder
- Substance use
- Other disorders as adults

- Has deliberately engaged in fire setting with the intention of causing serious damage
- Has deliberately destroyed others' property (other than fire setting)
- Has broken into someone else's house, building, or car
- Often lies to obtain goods or favors or to avoid obligations
- Has stolen items of nontrivial value without confronting a victim
- Often stays out at night despite parenting restrictions, beginning before age thirteen
- Has run away from home overnight at least twice, or once without returning for a lengthy time
- Is often truant from school, beginning before age thirteen

At least three of these criteria must have been present over the past twelve months, with at least one being present in the last six months. The behaviors must also be causing significant impairment in daily functioning.

The severity of symptoms in a child with conduct disorder varies. Each child is a unique individual and has had different life experiences that account for some of the symptoms seen with this disorder. The qualifying symptoms that your child displays may be considered as severe, moderate, or mild.

Children who suffer from conduct disorder display symptoms such as having difficulty establishing healthy relationships and showing empathy for others.

Self-preservation by looking out for only themselves and showing aggression toward others, animals, and property is also demonstrated. In addition, they are typically feared and frequently use bullying tactics to make others hang around with them.

Counselor's Corner

Fear

Sadly enough I have met numerous parents, caregivers, and teachers who have expressed fear of a child due to their behaviors.

I understand fear. It can be a very powerful factor in motivating one to do something or not to do something. Don't allow any fear that you have of a defiant, or perhaps conduct disorder child push you toward getting help for them and for yourself.

The symptoms of conduct disorder make it hard for these children to find their place in a world dependent on relationships with others and obedience of laws. Safety of the child and others is a concern. Prompt treatment is needed.

Children with conduct disorder have similar control needs as those diagnosed with oppositional defiant disorder and need many of the same parent supports. If you haven't already, take time to read the beginning of this chapter on oppositional defiant disorder.

Although many of the strategies already presented previously may have a positive impact on your child who has a diagnosis of conduct disorder, there are five that have the potential to have the greatest impact. Combining these with supportive mental health counseling and community services will give your child the best opportunity for managing conduct disorder.

Interventions

1. Practice appropriate social interactions. Children who have a diagnosis of conduct disorder will resist social skill training. Whether offered by caregivers, through the school, or though mental health counseling, your child is likely to resist. Children who are diagnosed with conduct disorder rarely view their behavior as troublesome. They see no reason to change and therefore will require intensive work from a provider who has much experience in this area.

    Work with your child's pediatrician and with the school counselor or social worker to gain community referrals for professional help. Upon reaching out to a prospective therapist, inquire into their specialties and how they can best help your child and family.

2. Conduct disorder is a serious diagnosis that can only be determined by a mental health or medical professional. Treating conduct disorder requires interventions from not only parents, but also community agencies, primary

care physicians, and all those who come into contact with your child.

3. Reinforce appropriate behaviors and do not harshly punish. No matter how small the gains, make it a point to recognize the positive choices that your child is making throughout each and every day. Hold firm to this intervention as your child will likely question if this strategy is here to stay by increasing some of their negative choices. This is because children with conduct disorder engage in controlling and manipulative behaviors.

    Testing the waters is part of all kids' development, but it is especially true with that of a defiant child. Never waver. Show your child how much you notice all the wonderful things they do. This will prove to be refreshing to your child as well as to you.

4. Find ways to increase emotional bonds between caregivers. A child bonds with his parents early in life. The older the child, the harder it will be to form a healthy bond. However, no matter the age of your child, take this opportunity and all the opportunities that are to come to be that parent who shows patience, caring, support, and love no matter what.

    This is not to say that you should always take your child's side. Tough love is part of the bonding equation. Being your child's friend first will only serve to increase the problems. Be a parent first and a friend second. This will greatly benefit your child as an adult.

    It is never too late to make changes for the better.

5. Provide academic help. Children diagnosed with conduct disorder also show behavior problems in school. Your child may be falling behind in their academics due to these difficulties. Arrange for a tutor to ensure that the school work gets done and to prevent your child from falling further behind. Falling behind makes your child feel frustrated

and different from the majority of their peers. As you can guess, this will trigger additional negative behaviors.

Tip: Resistance here is to be expected. Instead of demanding your child to work with a tutor, which will not work, create a plan together to decide how getting their school work done will happen. Considering their opinion in a big decision like this is important. If further help is needed, reach out to a mental health professional or to community agencies for support.

6. Visit behaviorcorner.com for more information and contact options for getting additional guidance from a professional therapist.

Disrespectful

Introduction

You will not get through life without someone being disrespectful to you. It is just reality. Humans have emotions, and sometimes those emotions get the best of us. We become frustrated, and this can lead to us showing disrespect to those around us. Although frustration is normal, it is not okay to treat others with disrespect. It will do your child good to learn this early on.

Gaining control, making a strong statement, jealousy, or whatever other reason people have for showing disrespect generally results in hurt feelings and damaged relationships.

> Every emotion is okay. It is what we do with those emotions that will make all the difference.

Showing your child how to treat others will take them far on the road of life. Having considerate social skills is a desirable trait for anyone to have.

The strategies below will help to decrease the amount of disrespect that your child is showing. As with learning any life skill, treating others respectfully is one that deserves constant reinforcement and correction when needed. We all make mistakes from time to time. One of your jobs as a parent is to support your child every step of the way to make positive future choices.

Formal Diagnosis

There is no formal diagnosis for disrespect alone. Although diagnoses exist with disrespect as a symptom, no diagnosis addresses disrespect as the sole symptom.

Interventions

1. Visit the Counselor's Corner at behaviorcorner.com to arrange for online counseling for you and your child.

2. Respectfully put an end to verbal battles by calmly saying, "This conversation is over. If you continue talking about it, you will [name the consequence]." Follow through on this and do *not* engage with your child on this topic again until you are both calm.

3. Unless it is an emergency, do not give your child what they are trying to get if they are yelling or being rude. A discussion about their needs and wants can occur when they are calm. State this fact calmly.

4. Treat your child with respect. Make a point to tell them and show them ways in which you show respect. Being a respectful role model will combine your words and actions to reinforce how to show respect back to you and to others.

5. Figure out what happened just before the disrespect occurred. Another consideration is to think about any life changes that have taken place lately that could be triggering an increase in disrespectful behavior. Answering these questions will help you to understand how to best address potential triggers to disrespect.

6. Establish and use negative consequences for disrespectful behavior. On the flip side, use positive consequences for respectful behavior. As always, be consistent in using both types of consequences for the best results.

    Tip: You will see the most results with this intervention if positive consequences are given more often than negative consequences.

7. Expect your child to apologize and to serve any other established consequence prior to participating in privileges. Keep in mind that most everything you allow your child to do is a privilege (talking on the phone, watching television, going outside, sitting in a favorite chair, etc.)

> Privileges are considered everything
> besides necessities such as food, water,
> shelter, clothing, warmth, and love.

8. Record your child being disrespectful. Show the video and reflect on how they sound and look. Are they proud? What would they like to see differently next time?

9. Correct any forms of disrespect in private and address your child's disrespect as soon as possible after the disrespect is shown. If you need to, remove your child from others (or ask the other people to leave the area temporarily) to discuss the inappropriate actions and to educate your child on how to handle the situation differently in the future. Again, your child should be willing to apologize.

10. Make sure that when you correct your child, they know specifically what they did that was disrespectful. Work with them to brainstorm different ways of getting their needs and wants met.

11. Do not hit your child. Even if they hit you as part of their disrespectful behavior, it is never okay to hit back. You may hold their arms to their side until they are calm, direct them to time-out, or walk away from the situation until they calm down enough to begin problem-solving and planning for future behaviors with you.

12. Use an "I" message to convey your feelings to your child. These statements are a very powerful way to let someone know how their actions made you feel without putting them on the defensive. The secret is in the use of the word "I" instead of "you."

    1. "I feel sad when you tell me to shut up. I would like you to speak to me using kind words."

        versus

    2. "You have to stop making me feel so sad. You cannot tell me to shut up any more. Stop doing that."

Do you see the difference between the "I" message that speak primarily about yourself? Everyone reacts better when presented with an "I" message. Choice number one is much more effective in communicating with others.

13. Communicate with your child's school and other caregivers about the interventions you are using to help decrease your child's level of disrespect. Ask them to use the interventions in their settings as well.

14. Remain calm and in control. Do not let your child see that they can get a rise out of you. If they do, they may feel as though they are the one in control and will continue to use this type of behavior.

15. Teach, model, and practice with your child ways to respectfully express their opinion.

16. Discourage your child from spending time with others who use disrespectful means to interact. Do not keep that type of company yourself either.

17. Be patient. Even if you feel that your child has mastered the art of respecting you and others, no one is perfect. Things happen and mistakes are made. Be prepared to support, teach, and reteach throughout your child's life.

18. Seize the moment. Begin addressing your child's disrespect today. If you think you have time to wait and figure that you will deal with your child's disrespect when they get older, you and your child will suffer.

Children learn the bulk of their foundational social skills, how to behave, and how to problem-solve when they are very young. Even before your child can talk, you need to encourage respectful interactions.

Some ways to foster respectful behavior in young children are the following:

- When your child tries to hit, calmly put their hands to their side and say "No" in a stern voice. No matter the age, do not hit back. If you do, your child will learn that hitting is in fact acceptable.

- When your child speaks to you in a rude tone of voice or tries to demand things of you, calmly state that it is not okay for them to speak to you like that. They must apologize and try again. If it continues, they must serve a negative consequence (usually a time-out) to think about how to handle that situation differently.

As you can imagine, these procedures are much easier to implement with young children. When you use these ideas consistently, your child will learn how to interact with others successfully. It is up to you to teach your child right from wrong. Starting early will have the greatest reward.

For those of you who don't have the gift of time, it is even more critical for you to use your consistency skills when giving consequences. You will find the most success in giving frequent positive consequences to your child as these will give the greatest motivation to succeed versus always getting a negative consequence. Refer to our first five chapters and appendix A for further advice.

Counselor's Corner

From Barb's house

When my kids were young, they learned very quickly about respectful behavior. In a very short time, all they needed was "the look" and they knew an apology had better be coming and a time-out would be given. Sometimes they even put themselves in time out. Needless to say, hitting and rude tones were few and far between in my home.

No one is perfect and just because we didn't have many of these issues, we had enough.....I'm right there with all of you!

19. Create and use a behavior plan that works to specifically address your child's disrespect. Establish the expectations of the plan with clear rules such as

    1. speaking in a calm tone,
    2. saying only kind things, and
    3. follow adult directions the first time.

    The expectations that are decided upon need to be followed by everyone in the home and reinforced consistently by all adults. Give all the children living in the home positive and negative consequences for their behavioral choices. Rewards received by one child will encourage another to earn the positive consequence as well.

20. Give plenty of positive acknowledgement when your child treats you and others respectfully. Tell your child specifically what they did that you are proud of. Give verbal praise sometimes and offer more tangible rewards during other times of success. These positive acknowledgements will increase your child's sense of accomplishment, self-esteem, and level of respect.

21. Stay calm and do not argue with your child. Arguing is disrespectful in nature. If you use yelling and arguing as a means to solve your problems, you child will learn that these things are acceptable.

22. Remove your child from a situation where they are acting disrespectfully. They may return once an apology is given and have a plan to change the behavior for the better.

23. Keep your child's routine as consistent as possible to avoid any surprises. Have homework, chores, dinner, and other activities at the same time each day when possible. Knowing what to expect will decrease the chance that your child will act out in a disrespectful manner.

24. Keep an open mind when your child requests a special privilege. For example, if they want to stay up late on a school night to watch a special television show, compromise by recording the program and allow them to stay up late to watch it on a nonschool night.

25. Visit behaviorcorner.com for more information and contact options for getting additional guidance from a professional therapist.

Disruptive Mood Dysregulation Disorder

Introduction

Many of you reading this may never have heard of this disorder. Or perhaps you are reading this chapter because someone you know was recently diagnosed with this disorder, maybe even someone in your family. Disruptive mood dysregulation disorder (DMDD) is a relatively new clinical diagnosis for children.

Research has shown that far too many children have been given diagnoses and treatment for disorders such as bipolar that didn't meet their true needs. The results of this have been children suffering from an unknown disorder and receiving treatment that hasn't helped them or their families to cope and rise above the symptoms of DMDD.

Formal Diagnosis

According to the American Psychiatric Association, disruptive mood dysregulation disorder is defined as thus:

- Severe repeated temper outbursts are demonstrated verbally (verbal rages) and/or behaviorally that are completely out of proportion in intensity or duration to the given situation or circumstance.
- The temper outbursts are not appropriate for the person's developmental level.
- The temper outbursts occur an average of three or more times per week.

- The person's mood between temper outbursts is continuously irritable or angry most of the day, nearly every day, and is observed by others.

Common Co-Existing Conditions

- Oppositional defiant disorder
- Attention-deficit/hyperactivity disorder
- Anxiety
- Depression
- Autism spectrum disorders
- Suicide risk
- Substance use

The symptoms described in the above bullets must be present for twelve or more months, with no more than three consecutive months void of showing all the symptoms. Additionally, the symptoms listed above must be present in at least two out of three settings (home, school, with peers) and be severe in at least one setting.

A diagnosis of DMDD should not be made prior to age six or after the age of eighteen. However, the age of when the symptoms first start must be before ten years of age.

Additional criteria for a diagnosis of DMDD are as follows:

- The person has never met the symptom criteria for a manic or hypomanic episode (see the "Bipolar" chapter for a comparison chart of manic versus hypomanic found in the bipolar chapter) that has lasted for more than one day.
- The temper outburst symptoms do not occur only during an episode of major depression disorder and are not better explained by another mental disorder.
- The symptoms are not due to the effects of substance use, another medical condition, or a neurological condition.

DMDD is difficult for everyone to manage. Improvement will take time, dedication, and patience.

It is normal and expected for children and adults to feel irritable and angry from time to time. When our children are feeling this way, we should strive to teach them how to cope with their feelings in order to make positive choices. One way we do this is by making positive choices ourselves when we feel upset. Although these times of irritability and anger are undesirable, we deal with them and move on. Children who suffer from disruptive mood dysregulation disorder struggle with the dealing and moving on parts. In addition, their inability to cope is viewed as extreme and occurs frequently.

The main symptom of being irritable and the resulting behaviors are difficult for parents, teachers, caregivers, and children alike to manage day in and day out. As a result, relationships with family members, caregivers, and peers are normally strained. Doing well in school is also seen as a challenge. Getting help and using the right interventions will work to ease this difficult time.

Be patient with each of the following interventions and with your child's progress. Disruptive mood dysregulation disorder isn't something that will be resolved overnight. It takes dedication, time, and patience.

Every day is a new day. Give your child the best of you! You will never regret it, even in the most challenging of situations.

Interventions

1. Keep in touch with your child's doctor and with a mental health therapist. These two professionals are the best people to have on your team. Working with people who come from a medical background and a behavioral background is what will benefit your child and family the most. Getting help for your child is critical.

2. Speak to your child's doctor or a child psychiatrist about medications that may be beneficial.

3. Set up individual counseling for your child. Your child will have the opportunity to learn and practice coping skills and social skills as well as increase their awareness to their

environment. Improved self-esteem, medication compliance, and overall improved functioning in daily activities
are further benefits to counseling. If you need referrals to
find a mental health provider, ask your child's doctor or
school counselor/school social worker.

4. Visit the Counselor's Corner at behaviorcorner.com to
arrange for online counseling for you and your child.

5. Take care of yourself. You have a lot going on in your "normal" life. When you add a child with DMDD to the mix,
things can easily get overwhelming. Rely on your support system of family and friends, and contact community
agencies to inquire about additional resources that may be
beneficial for your child and/or family.

6. Ask questions. Talk with the professionals working with
your child about what they know about DMDD and the
treatments available. Be open to getting a second opinion
and then make the best choice for your child. Having the
facts can bring you confidence in making treatment decisions for your child.

7. Create a behavior plan. (See appendix A.)

8. Consistent behavior plans and strategies must be applied
across all settings of your child's day and with each caregiver to be most effective.

9. Be proactive by establishing consequences before problems
occur. This allows your child to have a greater understanding of what the outcome will be of their actions. Providing
your child with this information gives them a *chance* and
a *choice* (two very important ways to empower your child)
when making their own decisions. After all, your child is
in charge of their own actions. Just be sure to implement
the positive and negative consequences consistently.

10. Expect your child to apologize and to serve any other
established consequence prior to participating in privileges. Keep in mind that most everything that you allow

your child to do (talking on the phone, watching television, going outside, sitting in a favorite chair, etc.) is a privilege.

> Privileges are considered everything besides necessities such as food, water, shelter, clothing, warmth, and love.

11. Discuss the interventions that are being tried at home, in school, and in the community with a mental health counselor. The counselor will be able to give their feedback on any changes that you may want to try along with things to keep doing. Having your child present when speaking about the interventions will be powerful in motivating them to respond positively.

12. Regularly work with your child's teacher(s) on a plan to manage irritability and outbursts in school. Allow school staff and the mental health provider to speak about the observations and how the interventions are working.

13. Create a system for frequent communication so that you know how the plan is working and so that your child knows that their teacher(s) and you are always working together. It is possible that your child will need a formal plan to be put into place depending on the severity of the DMDD. If this is the case, contact the principal of the school and the director of special education to get that process going.

14. Always work with your child on how to cope with strong feelings. Never stop doing this and never stop practicing. It will be frustrating during the times when your child chooses not to use the skills, but keep practicing anyway. Things will improve in the long run. | Never, ever give up

15. Make sure your child's basic needs are met. Hunger, thirst, feeling tired, being too hot or too cold, or feeling uncared for greatly adds to experiencing irritability and anger.

Tip: When you leave the house, bring along a drink and a snack. Being prepared just in case will make everyone happy.

16. Give nonverbal recognition to your child when you observe good behavior. This can include a sticker, a smile face on a piece of paper, written words of encouragement, a hug, a thumbs-up, or whatever else you can think of.

17. Negotiate with your child to decide on the number of times they think they will lose their temper. Provide that exact number of tangible items on a checklist or with chips, scraps of paper or fabric, beads, cereal pieces, candy, etc. One item must be turned in each time your child displays an outburst. Keep track of the number remaining at the end of the day in order to show progress. Extra items may be turned in for a reward or eaten (edible token items).

18. Regularly catch your child using positive behavior and tell them what specifically makes you proud.

19. Encourage your child to participate in daily physical activity. This helps to work through strong emotions and can help the brain improve its processing and problem-solving abilities.

20. Regularly encourage your child to focus their energy on taking control of themselves. Empowering children to make choices to achieve what they want in life is extremely valuable. With this skill they can move beyond just focusing on consequences linked to their behavior to considering the outcomes that they are choosing based on their actions and decisions.

21. If communicating with their words is hard for your child, develop a plan where you both agree on nonverbal signals that indicate when frustration or anger is being felt. Once the nonverbal signals are used, your child can then engage in agreed-upon calming activities or can go to a quiet place to deal with their feelings. Be sure that the development of this plan occurs when your child is calm.

22. Once an outburst has ended and your child is calm, give them encouragement to state their feelings, accept their feelings, and discover the primary feeling or cause. Ask them what they can do if it happens again. Also, ask what can be done now about the situation.

23. Reinforce that irritability and anger are natural emotions. Practice the positive choices to deal with anger found in appendix C. If your child is unwilling to engage in this conversation and practice with you, find a mental health therapist or community support system that they can participate in. Fostering this learning must be done now. Learning new ways of coping becomes harder as your child gets older.

24. Be a positive role model to teach your child how to manage emotions and how to get their needs met. Children watch our every move as they figure things out. Let them see how you want them to behave.

25. Teach your child that becoming angry and having an outburst does not solve problems. Teach the following problem-solving steps:

    • Identify the problem.
    • Develop a list of solutions.
    • List the pros and cons for each solution.
    • Pick the best solution.
    • Evaluate.

Counselor's Corner

Post it

Post the steps to solving problems on a white board, chalk board, or on anything else where your child can be reminded of the steps to take. The greatness about having it on a whiteboard or chalkboard is that they will be able to brainstorm each step on the spot!

Post each step by leaving enough space in-between so they can write their ideas.
Brilliant!

26. Help your child express their feelings by using their words. (I feel _____ when _____. I need _____.)

27. When planning for future positive decisions, role-play with your child so that they have a chance to practice and to become fully prepared.

28. Encourage your child to refocus their energies on something that is enjoyable in order to calm down or to prevent an outburst.

29. Use visuals such as pictures or sign language to help redirect your child when becoming frustrated so that the amount of verbal words are as few as possible. Talking to a child can quickly create an overwhelming situation.

30. Never ignore statements that your child says about suicide, harming himself, or harming others. Take these statements seriously and get your child help.

31. Don't overreact when your child displays extreme symptoms.

32. Try your best to have a calm state of mind. This will help you to think more clearly and will help to calm your child as well.

33. Help your child to become aware of their rights and the rights of others by teaching them about empathy.

Teaching empathy does us all good.

34. Teach your child conflict resolution skills, assertiveness skills, problem-solving skills, and stress management techniques.

35. Use social stories to teach coping skills, problem-solving skills, and to help your child understand the connection between behavior and consequences. For more information on this, visit www.thegraycenter.org

36. Always be patient as children will need regular reminders of their choices.

37. Provide daily structure, routine, and consistency. Your child will be able to handle daily expectations better when they know what to expect.

38. Provide a safe and quiet area that your child can use as a time-away spot. This could be a under a table covered with a blanket or in a big box with holes. Be creative and ask for your child's input about what they feel would help the most.

39. Choose your battles carefully. There are some things that truly do not need to be addressed. Consider the end result of addressing an issue versus just letting it go. Use your judgment wisely.

40. Establish a behavior modification program where your child earns privileges instead of losing them. A great way to do this is to reward positive behavior with points or tokens. These tokens/points can be turned in for agreed upon privileges. Here are a few points of special note:

    • When a negative consequence needs to be given, the points/tokens are off-limits and cannot be used until your child has served the consequence.
    • Never take away points or tokens that are already earned.
    • This type of behavior system allows for your child to earn privileges and to avoid feeling defeated by losing privileges previously earned.

41. Help your child learn how to control their actions by teaching them to identify their triggers and options for coping.

42. Document your child's moods and behavior choices. List the time of day, duration of symptoms and behaviors, and what occurred immediately prior to and after the behavior. Reflecting back upon this data can be very helpful when making behavior plans for your home and when working with outside professionals.

This can also be beneficial for you to identify what may be triggers for your child and what you can put into place as a preventative measure instead of reacting after it is too late.

43. Recognize your child's accomplishments and be positive whenever possible.

44. Discipline appropriately. This includes

- clear and simple communication of behavioral expectations,
- setting appropriate limits,
- monitoring and supervising your children's behavior carefully, and
- providing positive attention and rewards or privileges for showing effort in meeting the expectations.

45. Do not give into tantrums, nagging, or aggression. If you do, your child will be encouraged to continue their defiance because the inappropriate behaviors paid off for them.

46. Teach your child social skills. These skills need to include empathy, anger management, dealing with disappointment, communicating feelings, problem-solving, and cooperating with others. See appendix D for ideas on teaching social skills to your children.

47. If your child takes medication, avoid connecting good behavior to medication. We are still responsible for our actions with or without medication.

48. Always give choices. These choices should be options that you and your child are comfortable with. By doing this

you are encouraging your child to make a positive choice while installing a feeling of control in making their own decisions. Since control is something that that is sought, this can be a powerful strategy.

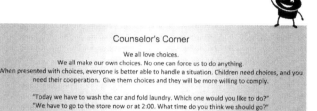

Counselor's Corner

We all love choices.
We all make our own choices. No one can force us to do anything.
When presented with choices, everyone is better able to handle a situation. Children need choices, and you need their cooperation. Give them choices and they will be more willing to comply.

"Today we have to wash the car and fold laundry. Which one would you like to do?"
"We have to go to the store now or at 2:00. What time do you think we should go?"

49. Give calm, clear, direct, and specific instructions Helpful tips for giving your children instructions include the following:

- Reduce your talk time; be specific, clear, and brief.
- Give only one instruction at a time.
- Allow at least ten seconds for your child to respond.
- Repeat an instruction no more than once; use a consequence if your child is still not responding. Do this every time! Being consistent with this one will teach your child that you mean business and that the only payoff received for not following directions is an undesirable consequence.
- Give instructions while using eye contact instead of shouting through the house.

50. When your child is agitated, it is critical to not overwhelm them. Feeling overwhelmed leads to further defiance and loss of trust in you as the parent to help. Here are some helpful tips for working with your child when they are upset:

- Give your child a reasonable amount of time to calm down.

- When speaking, use a calm voice. Do not do this in front of others. Privacy is important. If your child continues to be agitated, give additional calming time.
- Always be available by saying, "If you need help, let me know."
- If your child becomes upset and is unable to complete a chore or task that you have requested, that task must be made up at a later time. This shows your child that they have responsibilities and that negative behavior responses will not relieve them of these responsibilities.
- Do not engage in a power struggle with your child and do not answer their questions while upset. These two things put your child in charge, not you.

51. Create your household rules with everyone present.

- Be willing to listen to everyone's opinion and to negotiate.
- Establish positive and negative consequences associated with each rule.
- Ensure that the rules and consequences are clearly stated.
- Post the rules and consequences as a reminder and a reference tool. This can be done by hanging them on the fridge or creating a poster.
- If you have young children, the use of pictures to remind them of the rules can be helpful.
- Uphold the rules consistently and without fail.

52. Once the expectations are established, revisit your household rules at least every other week.
53. The entire family should use role-playing activities to practice the rules and expectations of your home. When full understanding of how to perform the rules is established, only then can a parent hold their children accountable for their behavior.

54. Always be consistent. Plan strategies that you can implement regularly.

55. Never ever call your children "bad." It is the behavior that is dissatisfying, not the child. Be sure to tell your child that they are *not* bad. However, the choices that were made are not what you expect. We can all learn from our mistakes and make better choices in the future. Calmly and lovingly supporting your children through this process will show how much you love them.

56. For every negative consequence, try to recognize your child in four or more positive ways. These times of recognition should be specific to the positive behavior you are seeing and contain details of what is being done right. Research has found that praise that is behavior-specific and delivered in a positive and genuine manner is one of the most effective tools for motivating people. Praise should always be immediate, frequent, enthusiastic, and descriptive, and it should be given by using eye contact.

57. Look at your child as a whole person. Each of us have strengths and weaknesses. Your child is no exception to this. Take some time to acknowledge their strengths.

> Each of us is a special person created to do special things. Along with all the greatness we possess, we have weaknesses. Accept your child's weaknesses and celebrate their strengths.

58. Encourage your child to monitor their own behavior by saying, "Tell me, what is terrific about what you are doing right now?"

59. When your child is doing something that could result in trouble, stop the activity and ask them what they're doing. Emphasize that your goal in this is to help to keep them from trouble.

60. Give consistent messages about what you expect and the positive and negative consequences associated with chosen behavior.
61. Encourage your child to become an expert on what they need to make the best choices.
62. Remind your child that they are in control of their own behavior; thus, the consequences received are based on their behavior, not yours.
63. Acknowledge your child's feelings and wants. Be willing to negotiate. This allows your child to feel that they have a voice as they strive for some independence.
64. Ask your child what they want.
65. Requests should be given using a firm, calm, quiet tone of voice and stated within approximately three feet of your child once eye contact has been established.
66. Allow your child to release anger through exercise or by working with clay, stress balls, or any other type of material and work out frustrations in an appropriate manner. These are wonderful ways to teach your child how to manage emotions.
67. When speaking with your child about their behavior, remember that humans are not motivated to change behavior that isn't seen as a problem. For change to happen, you and your child must see a need and feel a desire to make the change.

Counselor's Corner

Humans in general will not make changes or be willing to change behaviors that they feel are not a problem.

Even if your child will not discuss future plans for managing feelings or situations, rest assured that you are sending a loving and supportive message when you offer your time to talk with them.

Keep on trying and do your best to stay consistent and supportive.

Even if it feels as though you are not getting through to your child, I guarantee you that they notice that you are trying and may one day take you up on your offer to open up.

No one says that parenting is an easy job. As a matter of fact, it is the hardest job on earth when done correctly!

Push forward my friend. Your rewards will be great.

68. When giving a first request, use the word "please" and give your child at least a ten-second wait time. If successful, give positive reinforcement. If your child does not comply, a second request is started with "You need to." Wait time is given and choices are offered. Reinforcement is given if your child complies. If there is no compliance, a consequence is given. This process *must* be used consistently.

69. Use a silly voice as a distraction tool to redirect your child's focus. No negative gestures or expressions should be used.

70. Say exactly what you want by keeping your requests and/ or explanations short and to the point. A good rule is to keep your communication within fifteen to twenty words. Long lectures will do no good.

71. Make requests to your child by deferring control. For example, "The clock says it is time to go" is heard very differently than your request of "It's time to go."

72. Be empathetic as you anticipate problems by saying, "I know this might be difficult…" This will prepare your child for what comes next. With your help, they can think about some ways to problem solve the situation even before it occurs

73. Ask your child how they would feel if their actions were to be seen in a movie or on television for all to see. Ask, "Would you feel proud?" or "What would you change?"

74. Work with your child and caregivers to try to identify what increases anxiety along with what their triggers may be for choosing negative behavior. Anxiety may play a role in negative behavior choices as your child struggles to process anxious feelings.

75. Teach your child to talk about their feelings instead of acting on them. Give them choices to use verbal words, written words, or drawings. Provide a safe place for your child to keep their written work until an established time when you two can look it over.

76. Develop a predictable daily schedule and give your child advanced notice if there are any changes. Predictability keeps anxiety, stress, and frustrations low.

77. Have fun and help your child feel good about their positive actions. Even though you may have to look hard to find them, I guarantee you that they exist. Keep looking!

78. Listen to your child before reacting. This makes them feel heard and valued. As a member of your family, they should be treated with respect just as you expect it from them.

79. Do not rehash a situation later in the day. When dealing with a behavior struggle, issue a consequence, plan for the future, and move on.

80. Be willing to walk away before a situation escalates.

81. Discuss problems privately. When in the presence of others, children feel the need to find control in the situation. They will try to exert that control especially when in the presence of others.

82. If medication is tried, it should be in conjunction with mental health therapy to gain the most favorable results. A method to gather data on the benefits and drawbacks of the medication should also be put into place.

83. When at home and a tantrum occurs, direct your child to the time-out place if possible and walk away. If it isn't possible, walk away from where they currently are. Make a statement that when they stop [insert behavior], you will talk with them about what they want. Be prepared to repeat this more than once. Beside this statement, nothing else should be said or done unless the situation is dangerous.

84. Prior to an activity where outbursts have been experienced in the past, remind your child of the expectations such as the use of identified coping skills, communication skills, and problem-solving skills.

85. Prepare your child prior to all activities of what the boundaries and expectations are. Regardless of there being a history of tantrums, it is good practice for any child to have reminders of the expectations in various situations.

86. Try to offer an alternative. When you must say no to your child, try to offer a comparable solution so they feel valued yet know they have to respect your decisions. For example, if you tell your child that they can't get candy at the store, offer them candy that you have at home after the next meal.

87. Visit behaviorcorner.com for more information and contact options for getting additional guidance from a professional therapist.

Does Not Listen

Introduction

This is one of the most common parenting concerns out there. I include myself in that category as well. You are not alone in your struggles and help is now at your fingertips!

Listening and actually doing what one is told are two very different things. We can listen to the words coming out of someone's mouth, but that doesn't mean that we will act on those words. The action part is a choice.

As parents, we would like our children to always choose to act upon our requests in an appropriate manner. Reality quickly pulls us back when we encounter daily struggles in this area.

> Getting upset with your children doesn't help. Kids can tune that stuff out anyway, especially when it happens a lot.

Whether your child is not paying attention to you, is being defiant, or doesn't seem motivated, you continue to be highly interested in them listening and following through on your requests. Believe me, I know!

For the sake of ease, the upcoming strategies use the phrases of "listening," "following directions," and "following through with your expectations" to indicate the action of your children doing what they are told. I have used several of these ideas consistently with my own children with success. Good luck.

Formal Diagnosis

There is no formal diagnosis identified for one who does not listen.

Interventions

1. Visit the Counselor's Corner at behaviorcorner.com to arrange for online counseling for you and your child.

2. Check that your child understands what you are saying. Do this by asking questions such as "What did I ask you to do?" or "Tell me what you heard me say."

3. Begin counting to three when your child does not listen after one reminder or warning. If you get to the count of three, it means that your child should receive a preestablished negative consequence, such as a time-out. Much of the time, you will find that you will only have to say "one" and your child will begin to follow through with your request.

    Tip: Your child must be aware of the process and know what will happen if you get to three *before* you try the counting method.

4. To the best of your ability make sure that all adults in your child's life are following the listening plan that you establish. Having common expectations in all areas of your child's day will result in faster behavior change.

5. Use eye contact each time you and your child speak to each other. This helps to make sure you have their attention. As an added bonus, when you use eye contact while talking, you are a role model on how to use this skill and its importance.

6. Remove all possible distractions when talking with your child. Turn the television off, no one else should be talking, you should not be texting, you should not be multitasking, etc. I know it is hard, but give it a try.

7. Keep you requests short. Use no more than fifteen to twenty words and keep it to one- or two-step directions. The less the better! It helps your child remember what you said because they only have to focus on what you are

saying for a very short time before starting the task. An example of a one-step direction is "I need you to brush your teeth, please." An example of a two-step direction is "I need to you brush your teeth and then get a book to read, please."

Tip: After a two-step direction, have your child repeat the key words of their task. Given the example above, you would prompt your child to say, "Teeth, book. Teeth, book. Teeth, book." Repeating these words will enhance your child's memory and help him focus on the task at hand.

8. Use "I" messages. Statements that begin with "I need you to…" are firm and clear actions statements. Your child will know exactly what you expect. Statements that begin with "I want you to…" also send a clear message but are not as firm.

   "I need" statements are best used with children who tend to manipulate situations. "I want" statements are best used with children who like to please adults. Either way, being clear and concise will increase the likelihood of your child listening to your expectations.

9. Consider your child's ability to follow through on what you are asking. They must be able to complete the tasks in order to find success.

10. Show your child how to do what you are asking. Complete understanding is the only way that your request will get done, and it is the only fair way to hold your child account-able. Modeling the action and role-playing are two very effective ways to accomplish this.

11. Be positive when making requests. Instead of saying "Stop hitting your brother," you could say "I need you to keep your hands to yourself please." Your request to cor-rect behavior should always have a positive action request (keep your hands to yourself). This tells your child exactly what you are requesting.

Hint: Think of an undesirable behavior that your child demonstrates. Now, create a positive action request and use it consistently. After some practice, slowly add more positive-action requests to address other behaviors. Before you know it, the majority of your requests will be phrased positively.

12. Do not talk down to your child or use threats. These two approaches lower self-esteem, teaches your child that these strategies are acceptable ways to get what they want, and will not end in an increased ability to listen.

13. Include an incentive for listening to your request. "After you take a bath, you may have a snack." State this in your *first* request so that your child does not learn that if they first refuse to do as you say, they will end up getting a reward (the snack).

14. Request that your child repeat back in their own words what you expect. Doing so will assist your child in processing your request at a greater level. In addition, you will be assured that they heard and understand your expectation.

15. Offer choices that serve to meet your expectations *and* give your child a sense of control and power. "I need you to empty the dishwasher or feed the dog. Your choice" or "Do you want to do your homework or chores first?" are two examples. Giving appropriate choices creates a win-win for everyone.

> Empowerment, control, and independence. Are you giving these things to your kids?

16. Discuss the consequences of your child's actions with them. If you have been consistent, they should already know what consequences are in store for them. This includes positive, logical, and negative consequences. Encouraging your child to understand the relationship

between these consequences and their behavior is critical for positive change.

17. Allow natural consequences to happen. This is the simplest way to teach your child responsibility. If they forget to bring their gym clothes to school, they can't play gym. If they leave their toys in the rain, the toys will get wet. These are not consequences that you are giving; this is what naturally happens in life—to all of us.

18. Make it your child's idea to listen to your request. We all perform better when it is our own ideas that we are fulfilling. Your child is included in that fact. Having positive consequences in place is an example of what can motivate your child to decide to listen—all on their own.

    Children (and adults) get excited to know that something positive awaits them. A positive behavior management program can do just that. (See appendix A for ideas to get you started.)

19. End the verbal exchange. When your child does not accept no for an answer, end the conversation as quickly as possible and stating, "I am not changing my mind. This conversation is over." Walk away after saying this. Ignore any more attempts that your child makes to reengage with you (unless they are being unsafe).

20. You must expect your child to follow your instructions each and every time. Allowing them to not listen on occasion sends the message that listening is optional. Mixed messages are confusing to understand. Not to mention, it will cause increased frustration for you because their lack of listening will continue.

21. Follow through on consequences—always. Following through teaches your child several things: trust, responsibility, and accountability, to name a few. When your child receives consistent responses from their behavior, the behaviors will change for the better.

22. Remind your child of their responsibility to follow your directions in all areas. Before they go somewhere such as school, the store, etc., ask them to tell you what their job is while out.

23. Be understanding of your child's feelings, yet stick to your expectations. "I understand that you are tired; however, I need you to complete your homework." Your child now knows that you are considering their feelings, yet they still have a job to do.

24. Give praise and rewards to other children in your home who are listening and following the expectations. Your child will want to gain positive consequences like the others have received and will strive to show improved behavior.

25. Consistently give negative consequences to your other children who fail to listen. This sends a powerful message to all that the rules apply to everyone.

Counselor's Corner

Run from L-A-Z-Y
The most harmful thing you can do to your child's listening progress is to get Lazy!
Two real-life examples of what l-a-z-y looks like:
- Letting your kids get away with inappropriate behaviors sometimes but not others
- Deciding not to give them a consequence that they earned because you are tired or in the middle of something

L-A-Z-Y equals much more work for you in the long-run and even more frustration for everyone.

There is no room for lazy or selfishness when you are a parent.

26. Remove your child from their audience if they refuse to follow directions while in the presence of others. Showing off is an attempt to get a rise out of others and/or an attempt to control the situation. Removing your child (or the audience) will quickly diffuse these behaviors. In addition to the removal, established consequences should be given for not listening.

27. Create a list of requests that need to be done such as chores and homework. Without your verbal prompts, your

child should be able to complete these requests just by looking at the list. Include your child when creating the list. Use visuals of the tasks and images that interest your child to make the list more appealing. Provide plenty of positive reinforcement for effort shown and even more for tasks completed.

28. Use your requests list at consistent times of day so that it becomes a part of your child's routine. Doing things at the same time each day helps us all to remember what needs to be done.

29. Visit behaviorcorner.com for more information and contact options for getting additional guidance from a professional therapist.

Does Not Take Personal Responsibility

Introduction

"Clean your room."

"Do your homework."

"Please remember to do your chores."

"Be home by 10:00 p.m. tonight and not a minute past."

"Be honest and stop blaming your brother."

"Keep your hands to yourself"

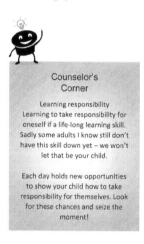

Counselor's Corner

Learning responsibility Learning to take responsibility for oneself if a life-long learning skill. Sadly some adults I know still don't have this skill down yet – we won't let that be your child.

Each day holds new opportunities to show your child how to take responsibility for themselves. Look for these chances and seize the moment!

Any of these sound familiar? I'm sure you can relate to at least one of these examples and can think of several others that you have said to try to get your children to take responsibility for themselves. However, if you are reading this, I have a feeling that those words haven't been as successful as you would have liked. We're going to work to change that right now!

For children to take personal responsibility for themselves, they must have a reason to do so. This is especially true while they are learning and developing this skill. For most children, being told that taking responsibly for themselves is the right thing to do will not create automatic use of this skill alone. However, their desire to do it will.

Desires dictate our choices. This, my friend, is human nature. Our desires are what motivate all of us. It only makes sense. Examples can include the following:

- If our children want a snack before bed, they will be motivated to eat their dinner.
- If you want to go on vacation, you will be motivated to save money.

Think about yourself in this moment. You are reading about increasing the likelihood of your child taking more responsibility for themselves. What is your desire in doing so? What is driving your choice in this moment? Now think about your child. What desires are encouraging them to make their choices?

See appendix A for a more in-depth reading on motivation, choices, and plans that will foster positive decision making.

Clearly, you want your children to start taking responsibility for themselves. So ask yourself, "What will motivate them to do so?"

If you haven't come up with a solid answer, let's do something about that. Read on.

Formal Diagnosis

There is no formal diagnosis to identify one who does not take personal responsibility.

Interventions

1. Visit the Counselor's Corner at behaviorcorner.com to arrange for online counseling for you and your child.
2. Provide clear directions, boundaries, and choices. At the same time, build in a motivating activity or object. For example, you can say, "You need to finish your homework before going out with your friends. Your curfew tonight is 9:00 p.m. It is up to you when you want to complete your homework.
3. Develop expectations with everyone in your home. These may include having specific times each day when home-

work is completed and/or that items are to be put away after use. Everyone must follow the rules. When the rules are being followed and rewarded, it will motivate others to do the same. See appendix A for more information.

For many children, it is extremely helpful to have a written list of expectations accompanied by a picture of your child completing the task. Also, next to each task should be a check box or a blank line for your child to mark off when the responsibility is completed. Not only does this give them independence to complete their job, it helps to keep them on track by checking items off as they go.

4. Start small by asking your child what they think they should be responsible for. Start with these items and slowly add others that your child can handle. Be consistent in your expectations of responsibilities so that they get comfortable and confident in completing them.

5. Remind your child frequently of their responsibilities and of the positive and negative consequences associated with following through or not. Review the expectations and *always* express your support and love for your child.

6. Teach and show your child how to complete each expectation. Practice with them to ensure understanding before you hold them accountable.

7. Praise and reward others in the home when they show responsible behavior and when they follow the household rules. Generally, children what to be included in the praise and the rewards that others are receiving. Therefore, they will strive to show responsibility themselves.

8. Be consistent each and every minute of every day. Consistency sends the message that you mean business; it sets boundaries and creates a safe environment for your child to begin showing responsible behavior.

9. Prepare/remind your child that they will have to take responsibility in a given situation before privileges can be earned. This may mean they have to tell the truth, clean up their mess, or pay back money earned through chores for a broken item prior to earning privileges.

10. Lack of taking personal responsibility is common and expected from young children. Consider your child's age and developmental level when seeking to increase their level of responsibility.

11. Allow for natural consequences to happen when possible. If your child doesn't complete their homework, they have school consequences. (Arrange a plan with your child's teacher ahead of time to ensure that this approach will work.) If your child leaves their toy in the rain, it may get ruined. Natural consequences are powerful teaching tools that take you out of the role of consequence-giver.

Counselor's Corner

Abilities

Natural consequence are wonderful if...your child can understand them.
Consideration must be given to your child's abilities before using any of the three consequences. Their age, development, and disabilities must be thought about when using consequences. If understanding and processing of how consequences link to behaviors is not possible, the effectiveness of the consequences will be non-existent.

12. Build in positive and negative consequences to any behavior plan used at home. Having consequences attached to expectations gives children a large amount of motivation to complete each item listed in the plan. See the "Must-Know Parenting Strategies" chapter for much more on how to use consequences to shape your child's decisions.

13. Celebrate your child's achievements and attempts to show responsible behavior. Your acknowledgement and rewards

given to your child is a huge reason for them to continue doing well.

14. Be specific. Tell your child exactly what you want from them. "Please put your truck in the green bin" or "It is time to do your homework. Please come to the table now" are examples of clear requests given to children to help remind them of their responsibilities.

15. Stick with one- or two-step directions. Giving your child too many items to be responsible for at one time will cause frustration and a decreased likelihood of your child being successful. Give clear and simple requests. Once your child completes the first request, praise them and tell them what the step is next. Completing one step and then listening to the next *is* showing responsibility.

16. Be a positive example. Ensure that you are demonstrating responsibility when in the presence of your child.

17. Revoke privileges until your child shows responsible behavior. This could include restricting time spent with friends when problems occur. It could also mean taking away items until your child can prove that they can be responsible with the items. Whatever the situation, just make sure that the privilege restriction is linked to the infraction.

> Privileges are considered everything besides necessities such as food, water, shelter, clothing, warmth, and love.

18. Work with your child to get them started on each task that is required of them. This is a good reminder of what needs to be done and also shows your support when you work with them. Be consistent each time, and your child will quickly learn what to expect.

19. If after several attempts at behavior planning and use of other interventions listed here your child continues to

show difficulty with taking responsibility for themselves, consult with their primary doctor and with a mental health professional. There could be a medical cause or a mental health issue that is hindering your child from finding success. Having an evaluation from both of these professionals will help to give you additional insight into your child's functioning and their abilities. They will also be able to further guide you in your parenting quest.

20. Visit behaviorcorner.com for more information and contact options for getting additional guidance from a professional therapist.

Encopresis

Introduction

Encopresis occurs when a child who has been toilet trained (typically over age four) has bowel movements in inappropriate places. Generally, these inappropriate bowel movements, a.k.a. "poop" as many of us commonly say to our children, happen in the child's clothes, which cause the clothes to become soiled.

Formal Diagnosis

According to the American Psychiatric Association, encopresis is diagnosed in the following instances:

- There is repeated passage of feces into inappropriate places, such as in clothing or on the floor. This passage could be seen as either involuntarily or intentionally.
- The inappropriate feces passage must occur at least once per month and continue for at least three months.
- The person must be at least four years of age or at a comparable developmental level.
- The behavior is not due to the effects of a substance or another medical condition, except for constipation that is not caused by another medical condition.

Common Co-Existing Conditions

- Anxiety
- Depression
- Behavior challenges
- Emotional difficulties
- Enuresis
- Oppositional defiant disorder
- Conduct disorder
- Attention-deficit/hyperactivity disorder
- Urinary tract infections and other medical conditions

If you are concerned that your child may have encopresis, take a look at these possible symptoms:

- Liquid-like stool in your child's clothing when they are not sick
- Frequent complaints of not feeling well
- Expressing discomfort with cramping or stomach pain
- Passing large stool that has a hard time going down the toilet
- Experiencing pain during bowel movements
- Decreased appetite
- Behavioral or emotional concerns

In the majority of cases, the cause of encopresis is medically based and termed as *constipation*. Constipation results in the feces becoming hard and highly uncomfortable to pass through the colon. As you can imagine, children choose to avoid the discomfort of passing large-sized feces by holding it in. This results in their colon enlarging and a loss of feeling that tells their brain to pass the stool.

Given all of that, perhaps you wonder where the soiling part comes into play. Well let me tell you.

What happens is that some stool manages to escape. Either known at that moment by the child or not, soft, liquid-like feces are released from the body around the hard stool. This is one cause of how stool enters the child's clothes. Thus, we have a case of medically based encopresis.

Another option to consider when piecing together the cause of encopresis could be environmental stressors. Occurrences such as the birth of a new sibling, being toilet trained too early, a move, illness, a parent obtaining new employment, and parents separating are possible examples. Sources of stress that cause emotional and/or behavioral problems have the potential to result in encopresis.

Regardless of the cause, there are many implications of this disorder. Therefore, it is important that you take action immediately to help your child.

Interventions

1. Get your child medical attention. Medical tests can easily and quickly determine if your child is in fact constipated through an abdominal X-ray. Medication to eliminate the presence of constipation is generally the medical intervention used if constipation is identified.

2. Provide your child with a mental health professional who can conduct an evaluation and provide counseling services. Whether dealing with a medically based case of encopresis or one caused by environmental stressors, a mental health counselor can assist with your child's feelings, family functioning, positive reinforcement planning, and he can also address social concerns that are present due to this disorder.

3. Visit the Counselor's Corner at behaviorcorner.com to arrange for online counseling for you and your child.

4. Ensure that your child gets plenty of daily exercise. A healthy body (including the bowels) demands exercise.

5. Be supportive and express unconditional love for your child. Encopresis can easily cause secondary symptoms such as embarrassment, low self-esteem, frustration, shame, and social isolation.

6. Take some time to visit encopresistreatment.com/. This website has reliable information plus easy-to-use resources.

7. Promote a diet that is high in fiber. Great high fiber choices include broccoli, popcorn, wheat bread, and fruit. Many grocery stores also carry fiber supplements for kids. These are a great way to make sure your child is getting enough. In addition to fiber, offer your child plenty of water throughout the day. Fiber intake and water go hand-in-hand to keep things moving. Fiber without water will not do the trick.

8. *Never* punish or criticize your child for soiling. This causes your child to feel alone, unloved, depressed, ashamed, and unaccepted. What they need is your help, not your criticism.

9. Be aware that your child may appear unfazed by soiling themselves. This could be due to denial or truly not knowing they have soiled their pants. Be patient and supportive *no matter what.*

10. Raising a child with encopresis can be extremely frustrating. Be sure that you are meeting your own needs along the way by relying on your support network to help you.

11. Establish a routine for your child to void stool. Consider having your child try to pass stool after the same meal each day. Consistent toileting times will help to regulate bowel movements. More importantly, it will help to reduce

the likelihood that your child will avoid passing their poop.

> Consistent avoidance not only results in further constipation, but it also stretches the colon and ultimately damages the nerve endings that are responsible for signaling your child's brain that it is time to poop.

12. Each time your child poops in the toilet, reward them. Give them praise and a physical reward for doing so. This may occur several times each day. Chart your child's successes so that they will be motivated to continue doing well. Once passing feces becomes regular, the use of rewards can be decreased.

13. Be consistent, positive, and optimistic in developing a successful pooping plan. Stick with it for several months and reevaluate regularly with your chosen providers and child. Even beyond the point of success, it is important to continue providing your child with an appropriate diet and encouragement to have regular bowel movements.

14. It is your positive support that will empower your child to beat encopresis. Without your support, love, and understanding, the prognosis is bleak.

15. Visit behaviorcorner.com for more information and contact options for getting additional guidance from a professional therapist.

Enuresis

Introduction

Enuresis is the act of urinating on oneself. It is common to hear about children with enuresis wetting the bed at night. Some of these same children may have wetting concerns during waking hours too. Whether a child is urinating while sleeping, awake, or both, it is a serious concern that must be addressed immediately.

Technically speaking, enuresis is categorized by two types, primary enuresis (PE) and secondary enuresis (SE). Enuresis has strong ties to genetics and is only diagnosed in those who are five years of age or older.

Primary enuresis occurs when a child has never established bladder control.

Secondary enuresis occurs when a child has achieved a minimum six-month period of continence (no wetting accidents) before the wetting begins.

Mental health problems are a common concern in children who experience either form of enuresis. This is typically due to the embarrassment, depression, anxiety, negative self-perception, poor relationships, poor school performance, low self-esteem and other personal consequences of enuresis.

Counselor's Corner

Get help for your child even if enuresis is not officially diagnosed. Emotional impairment can exist in children who experience wetting accidents as infrequent as once a month.

Primary enuresis is normally treated as a developmental delay that children typically grow out of. Only a small percentage of cases have a true medical cause.

Secondary enuresis appears to begin in response to a major life change such as parents divorcing, the birth of a new sibling, or any other large adjustment that children are forced to make. Secondary enuresis is also seen when children have a medical need such as a urinary tract infection.

Unfortunately, children with enuresis are frequently punished and are at high risk of emotional and physical abuse. Punishment has *no* place when responding to incidences of enuresis. It is not effective and is actually damaging to your child.

A good thing to keep in mind is that enuresis normally resolves on its own, especially if the child has had success at staying dry few times per week. If this is the case, medical professionals may choose to delay treatment interventions.

When treatment is agreed upon, the best predictor of a positive outcome rests with the child being ready, having supportive parents, having a positive attitude, and having the motivation to stay dry. Sadly, it is common for children to believe that they will never be dry. However, an optimistic outlook should be regularly encouraged.

Common Co-Existing Conditions

- Attention-deficit/hyperactivity disorder
- Low self-esteem
- Behavior concerns
- Emotional difficulties
- Sleep difficulties
- Developmental delays
- Encopresis
- Urinary tract infections and other medical conditions

Formal Diagnosis

According to the American Psychiatric Association, enuresis may be diagnosed when a person

- repeatedly voids urine into their bed or clothes (either involuntary or intentional);

- these symptoms happen twice a week for at least three consecutive months or have a significant impairment on the child's daily life and functioning;
- the person is at least five years of age or is at the comparable developmental level of that age; and
- the behavior is not due to the effects of a substance or another medical condition.

Interventions

1. Get advice from a medical doctor and a mental health professional, especially when your child reaches a social age (normally around five to six years old). A thorough medical examination will be completed and a developmental history of your child will be gathered to obtain all the necessary information for helping your child and family.

   Be sure to ask about what things you can do to best manage your child's needs and your own.

2. Treatment is primarily based on protecting your child's emotional wellness. Since the majority of enuresis cases resolve on their own, treatment to protect your child's self-esteem and emotional well-being are the priority. If your child struggles with a medically based case of enuresis, their emotional health along with their medical needs should be address simultaneously.

3. Visit the Counselor's Corner at behaviorcorner.com to arrange for online counseling for you and your child.

4. Visit www.dryatnight.com/ for information, resources, and treatment from an authority on enuresis.

5. Use a chart to track your child's progress toward increasing their dry time. Charts can be helpful to motivate children to stay dry during waking hours only. However, most cases are considered nocturnal enuresis (wetting only at night). In these circumstances, a motivational chart will not be useful and can actually make your child feel twice

as discouraged. Once when they wake up wet and again when they see on their chart that they didn't stay dry while sleeping. It isn't fair to hold a child accountable to something while they are sleeping.

6. Develop and use a behavior plan to help encourage positive behaviors. These are behaviors that we would expect from our children whether they have enuresis or not. Appendix A has many great ideas on behavior planning.

What does a behavior plan have to do with enuresis you ask? Children suffering the effects of enuresis (low self-esteem, poor social relationships, etc.) typically benefit from regular encouragement to make positive choices. A behavior plan can help to positively reinforce these things, especially when they experience success and feel good about it.

7. Family members or friends who have experienced enuresis should share their experience and offer emotional support to your child. Your child can be comforted by the fact that they know others who have had enuresis and who have overcome this disorder. This can help them feel less alone and instill hope.

> Punishment has *no* place when responding to incidences of enuresis. It is not effective and is actually damaging to your child.

8. Do *not* punish or criticize your child—ever! Yelling, punishing, hitting, name-calling or any other form of punishment will harm your child's self-esteem and the relationship that you two have. Instead of punishing or giving a consequence, use strategies to put a plan in place.

9. Always, always have patience. It will be hard spending the extra money on clothes, training pants, laundry soap, waterproof mattress covers, etc. It will also be hard giving up sleep at night to help your child get clean and to change a bed. Enuresis is something that a lot of kids struggle with. Show your patience and love every step of the way. It

will make enuresis so much easier to handle. Besides, getting upset and losing your cool won't help make anything better anyway.

10. Ask your family members or close friends for support during this time. Asking for help with the laundry or just for a break can do wonders. Remember the village we spoke about in the introduction? Use it.

11. Provide your child with daily opportunities for exercise. Keeping healthy and in shape is important for overall health. It also makes kids feel good about themselves because they have fun running around and playing.

12. Your child should never get to the point of being overtired. An overtired child has many more difficulties controlling their body's actions, including staying dry.

13. When needed, allow your child to use a big-kid diaper or training pants to prevent embarrassment and to reduce the negative impact on daily social functioning. Try not to rely too heavily on these though as your child may become accustomed to using them instead of using the toilet.

14. Have sleepovers at your house. When your child is old enough for sleepovers, offer to host them at your home. This will help your child feel more comfortable and any accidents can be handled discreetly.

15. Especially for nocturnal enuresis, restrict the amount of fluid intake your child has before going to bed, but allow plenty throughout the day.

16. Inquire about getting your child an enuresis alarm. Just as your child begins to wet, the alarm will sound alerting your child that they need to get to the bathroom.

17. Use a strict toileting schedule to help avoid wetting accidents. Be sure to have your child use the toilet before starting new activities, before the leaving home, before bed, and every couple of hours in between. Provide a reward for urinating on the toilet and use a chart to keep track of each time urine is produced on the toilet.

18. Write a note to your child's teacher and school nurse to allow your child bathroom usage as per the toileting schedule being used at home. As needed, bathroom requests need to be granted as well.

    If a medical note is required, contact your child's doctor immediately. Children need to use the toilet as soon as they feel the need to go and also per their plan instead of sticking to the school's schedule for bathroom breaks.

19. Consistent follow-up with all the professionals working with your child is important in order to gauge how treatment is going.

20. Be your child's cheerleader and advocate through this time. Your support, unconditional love, and acceptance will be a great motivator toward success.

21. Visit behaviorcorner.com for more information and contact options for getting additional guidance from a professional therapist.

Executive Function Disorder

Introduction

Although not recognized as a mental disorder by the American Psychiatric Association, executive function disorder is caused by a processing deficit in the brain. This can make tasks such as concentration, planning, organizing, remembering details, figuring things out, managing time, and respecting personal space difficult.

Executive functioning is needed to help us make sense of and apply our past experiences to our current and future decisions. Since learning from our past requires memory, planning, and organization within our brain, it isn't always easy for those who suffer with executive function disorder to be successful with this task.

Guided with valuable input from parents, teachers, speech therapists, and other providers, a mental health professional or your child's primary medical doctor can conduct an evaluation to determine your child's level of executive function skills.

Normal development of executive function skills are as follows:

- One year of age: Your child gives attention to a task voluntarily and shows interest in activities.
- Two to five years of age: Memory, ability to pay attention, and ability to plan their actions increases gradually.
- Five to six years of age: Your child should be able to easily follow a two-plus-step direction.
- Six years of age: Your child's brain is able to perform planning tasks by thinking before acting. Although not perfect, this skill is on the increase.
- Eight to ten years of age: Your child greatly increases their ability to pay attention and concentrate. Attention to detail and a desire to maintain accuracy is present.

Independent decision-making increases by considering and applying their past learning experiences with current situations.

- Ten to eleven years of age: Your child has adult-like abilities to control impulses and maintain attention. They can successfully test hypotheses and switch from one task to another without an issue.

Due to the high demand for attention and work completion in school, the majority of the following interventions need to be implemented during the school day. It is highly important that adults at school and at home work together in the planning process to address executive function needs. To do this, meet with your child's teacher regularly to address current needs and the effectiveness of interventions.

You are your child's best advocate.

Formal Diagnosis

Executive function disorder does not exist as a formal diagnosis from the American Psychiatric Association. Nonetheless, deficits in executive functioning affects many children and adults.

Interventions

1. If your child is of school age, be on the lookout for the following signs that may indicate an executive function weakness. Inquire about these signs with your child's teacher(s) and others who interact with your child daily.

   Special note: Although most children begin their school career at age five, the majority of these skills are not developmentally expected of a child prior to the first or second grades:

   - Completes school work but forgets to hand it in

- Written work is often incomplete or disorganized
- Has a hard time remembering information that was previously learned
- Has a hard time following and keeping track of directions
- Difficulty with transitioning from one activity to another
- Does not catch careless mistakes
- Has a hard time with regulating emotions
- Has a hard time monitoring personal behavior
- Requires more adult support and reminders than peers
- Has a hard time keeping track and organizing belongings
- Has inconsistent grades and work quality
- Cannot set personal goals
- Difficulty with time management
- Difficulty with planning
- Difficulty getting started with a task
- Difficulty solving problems
- Has a hard time completing tasks independently
- Shows signs of impulsivity
- Cannot estimate how much time has passed while engaged in an activity

2. Contact your child's doctor and arrange for your child to see a mental health professional. These two professionals can work together and may identify your child as having executive function concerns. Having this information will make it much easier to get your child's needs met during the school day. This is because formal documents that mandate individual strategies for students require that the child have a medical or mental need.

   Additionally, using the following interventions under the guidance of a mental health provider will make them even more effective and will help you to stay on track.

3. Visit the Counselor's Corner at behaviorcorner.com to arrange for online counseling for you and your child.

4. In order to be a positive and supportive family member, you must deal with your own feelings about your child having executive function difficulties. Gain knowledge and support from others in helping your manage your feelings and level of acceptance.

   None of this is your fault or your child's fault. Your child needs you. You can be their greatest asset in navigating through this disorder.

5. Speak directly with your child instead of addressing several family members at one time. Giving direct instructions and praise will result in greater success. Ask your child's teacher to do the same.

6. Be flexible and patient—always!

7. Do your best to role-play social situations with your child. Children with a weakness in executive function skills tend to be overly sensitive, impulsive, and/or talk too much. Be patient throughout this process as you keep in mind that your child may not possess these skills yet. Teach them and practice with them regularity. Use real-life examples if possible as you reflect and "redo" social situations that you observe.

Counselor's Corner

The scoop on social skills.
Social skills are needed in just about every aspect of life. Communicating with others, solving problems, reading body language, etc. are all examples of social skills.
To be successful in life, our social skill set must be strong.

Along with your own observations, ask your child's teacher(s) or caregivers for positive actions that they have witnessed along with areas of need. Praise your child for their strengths and practice the weaker skills regularly

8. Your patience must be strong. It takes a lot of work and time to see changes. Your child is worth it so stick it out. You will be happy you did. Children who don't receive the necessary supports are at risk for developing emotional, behavioral, and self-image problems as they get older.

9. Encourage your child to always try their best. This can be difficult because children tend to give up when they see inconsistent results from their efforts. An example of this is receiving a 100 percent on a spelling test one week and a 30 percent the next.

10. Work closely with your child's teachers(s) to implement a plan for school success. Your child may benefit from a visual plan being used in school, organization and work completion interventions, a personal schedule, daily communication between school and home, etc. Examples are included in appendix A.

11. Arrange for your child to have access to focus tools during the school day. These could include frequent breaks to stretch or get a drink, visual reminders to focus placed on their desk, close seating to the teacher, and seat movement opportunities such as bouncing their feet on a large rubber band or a bungee cord tied to the two front legs of his desk. Paying attention can be very difficult when a child is struggling with executive deficits. See the intervention section of chapter eight for more strategies to tame impulsive actions.

12. A fun way to encourage your child to focus is to set a timer at various times throughout the day. When the timer goes off and your child is focused on the task at hand, a positive consequence is given.

13. Ensure that your child has received a thorough evaluation. There are many overlapping disorders that commonly exist alongside executive functioning deficits.

Additionally, if learning problems are present, your child will likely experience failure despite their best efforts to succeed. Work with the school to get a full educational evaluation completed in order to assess your child's learning abilities.

14. Insist that your child be allowed to use a color-coded system that includes folders, binders, bins, or whatever else is needed to help with organization and their ability to process the environment. Be sure to label items with words and identifying pictures.

It is extremely important that your child is excited about this and understands how it works. If there is confusion or a lack of buy-in, this strategy will not help your child succeed.

15. Provide motivators. These motivators could be earning stickers on a chart, tokens, or points to be used to "purchase" privileges or items. Motivators like these help to support your child as it reminds them and gives them reasons to stick with a task. For more ideas, see appendix A.

16. Keep a set of school materials at home so that there is a back-up plan if your child forgets to bring something home.

17. Teach and reteach organizational skills. Through this process, you must provide continual reinforcement. Kids with executive function deficits must relearn skills until they become automatic. Support and practice allows executive functioning skills to develop to their greatest extent.

18. Your child must use a homework agenda (usually provided to each student by their school) so that everyone is aware of nightly homework assignments. Ask the teacher(s) to check that the agenda is filled out correctly before your child leaves school each day. Once independent in this task, request that the teacher(s) check it only periodically unless problems begin to arise again.

19. If your child is spending lengthy amounts of time completing homework every day, request a meeting with the teacher(s) about homework becoming modified. Many teachers agree that it is not necessary to do twenty of the same type of problem. As long as teachers can measure your child's ability in a few of the problems, they are normally satisfied that the skill has been learned.

    The amount of time normally required for homework varies depending on the age of your child. You can expect elementary children to have twenty to forty-five minutes of homework a night. In the older grades, estimates of one to two hours are the average.

20. Prior to doing homework or any other activity that requires seat time, allow them to engage in activities to burn energy. This could be running, exercise, or any other motor activity your child enjoys.

21. Assign chores based on your child's ability. Work together to show them how to complete a chore and be patient with their level of completion.

22. Use a daily calendar to label what will happen today. Talk about the unknowns such as "If it rains…"

Counselor's Corner

Disappointment

Let's be honest, we all want things to go our way and as scheduled. Regardless of a disability, deficit, or disorder, it is nice to be prepared for the possible "What ifs" in life.

Now that we all agree, try your best to prepare your child. This shows respect and gives wonderful examples of problem solving. Occasionally, "what ifs" creep in without forethought to prepare your child. In these cases, use past examples of schedule changes and how they were handled to point out how everything turned out just fine.

23. Regularly speak with your child about planning for future situations and how to use problem-solving methods to be successful. Use words and a lot of visual pictures to help keep your child on track.

24. Set realistic expectations and regularly reward accomplishments, even if they are small. If set expectations are not regularly being met, they are probably unrealistic or the child needs more support to reach the goals. Prioritize and choose your battles.

25. Give your child support and guidance when needed to complete a task. When the task is done, provide a nontangible reward such as a hug, a high five, or praise.

26. Provide consistent boundaries and a high level of structure.

27. Make sure your household rules are clearly stated and that your child has a full understanding of how to uphold the rules.

28. Establish no more than two goals or skills to work on at a time. Too many new skills can cause your child to become overwhelmed and resist the learning process.

29. Work together to develop the incentives that your child can earn in order to keep them motivated.

30. Establish a set time for organization each and every day.

31. Have fun with practicing skills through creative role play. One way to do this is to reverse roles. Allow your child to be the adult and you say, "Teach me how to stay focused" (or any other skill that your child is working on) and then switch roles. See appendix A for easy-to-use plans that help your child to stay focused. Additionally, the "Attention, Impulsivity, and Hyperactivity" chapter has many interventions on how to help a child learn to focus.

Counselor's Corner

How do you teach someone to focus?

To begin, your child must feel the need to increase their focus abilities. Understanding why they need to learn and use focus strategies will make the results of everyone's efforts positive and lasting. Give some of these a try:

- Repeat key words with your child so they remember what they need to do. These words should be repeated in your child's head until their task is done.
- Allow your child wiggle or stretch time before starting a task.
- Allow your child to take a break during tasks to wiggle, stretch, get a drink, or anything they need to restart their job. Give them approximately five minutes to do so.
- Provide your child a visual list so they can refer back to it independently.
- Give your child a timer and challenge them to beat the set time.
- Keep items in consistent places to reduce your child trying to find things they need.
- Give your child a small hand-held focusing tool to squeeze and help them to focus.
- Specifically praise focus behaviors that your child uses.

32. Help support your child by

- informing them of changes in the routine,
- allowing for breaks if they are having a hard time dealing with change and as needed,
- teaching relaxing self-talk skills,
- giving warnings of a transition prior to it happening,
- writing and regularly reading social stories about how to manage current situations and/or how to use social skills,
- providing social skills training,
- giving plenty of positive reinforcement for handling change,
- minimizing clutter, and

- scheduling a weekly time to organize and reflect on progress and skills.

33. Play Legos with your child. Focusing on Legos helps to support your child's ability to pay attention and develops flexible thinking along with organization and planning abilities. Deciding how many blocks are needed, planning out how to build their project, and sticking to it until done are all great abilities that foster life skills. What can be better than playing with your child while helping them learn? Have fun!

34. Use visuals with your child. Pictures on charts, index cards, the fridge, or anywhere else for your child to see will provide them with cues and reminders for what their responsibilities are. Create a routine chart to use daily. It is most helpful if each task item is listed using words and pictures.

    A personal checklist helps to foster independence and supports developing organization skills. Be sure that your child is capable of completing each task before you expect them to comply. If they can't complete the tasks, your child is only being set up to fail. You will both become discouraged and no growth will be seen.

    > Visuals are a huge help. Children who see a picture of something and then hear (or read) words that match the picture, have a much better chance at understanding what is expected.

    Tip: Take a picture of your child completing each task and paste it next to the written words. Pictures allow your child to understand what is expected rather than just trying to process the words. Listing the approximate length of time associated with completing each task can make it even more effective.

    For example, your child's morning checklist could include items such as the following:

    - Get out of bed when your alarm sounds (two minutes).

- Get dressed (three minutes).
- Use the toilet (one minute).
- Wash your hands and face (two minutes).
- Brush your teeth (two minutes).
- Brush your hair (two minutes).
- Sit down at the kitchen table (one minute).
- Eat breakfast (fifteen minutes).

Don't forget to use pictures of your child completing these tasks and make sure each task has a place to mark that it is complete.

Use this every day to help keep your child organized and independently responsible.

35. Give your child one-step directions. Only increase this to a two-step direction when they have been consistently successful.

    This strategy can also be used when your child has a multi-step project or a multi-step responsibility to complete. Separating out each step will be beneficial to your child's learning and will increase their ability to find success.

36. Provide your child with options but make them few. Children (and adults) enjoy having a say in the decisions they make. We all like to feel as though we have some control over our situation. As a guideline, present your child with no more than two choices at a time. Limited choices let your child's brain process and organize the information into a choice that they desire without becoming overloaded with options.

37. Teach your child how to use organizers, computers, tablets, watches, alarms, and other tools that can help them to stay focused. This will work to foster pride in independently accomplishing tasks.

38. Review plans and checklists daily.

39. Give your child advanced warning before a new activity will begin. Whether they need to stop what they are doing to eat dinner, go to the store, or take a shower, letting them know five minutes and again at two minutes before they have to change activities will be helpful. Using a timer seems to give this strategy even more power.

   Tip: For young children, use a transition puppet to tell your child when the activity will change. Your child can then carry this puppet (or another prized item) with them to their next activity.

40. Visit behaviorcorner.com for more information and contact options for getting additional guidance from a professional therapist.

Immature

Introduction

Innocence is something to be treasured. I used to ask myself, "Why are we rushing kids to grow up?" The answer awaited me as my work with children and families grew over the last decade.

I sadly learned that if kids don't mature on par with their peers, they are subject to potential criticisms, exclusion, and many social difficulties. None of these things are acceptable. The immature child needs to be supported in developing their social skills and taught how to effectively problem-solve tough situations.

Social skills are needed to succeed in just about every area of life. The immature child needs a hero to teach and support them. You can be the hero that can help them become a productive member of society.

Social skill deficits are what we see as the overriding issue that points to immaturity. At the heart of this immaturity, we commonly find children who are seeking attention, trying to fit in, and/or lacking in the knowledge of how to effectively behave at age-appropriate levels.

To assist in narrowing down possible reasons why your child is acting in immature ways, ask yourself (and your child) how their behavior is paying off for them. Finding out what the driving force is behind the immature behavior is a tough task, but it is a worthwhile one.

Whatever the potential reasons, the interventions listed in this chapter may help.

Be your kid's hero.

Formal Diagnosis

There is no formal diagnosis to identify one who lacks maturity.

Interventions

1. Visit the Counselor's Corner at behaviorcorner.com to arrange for online counseling for you and your child.

2. Focus on areas that your child is good at in order to promote success and to improve their self-esteem. This can help to improve their confidence and self-respect as well.

3. Observe your child in a variety of settings to determine where they have the most strength and the most needs. This will help you to zero in on what skills they need the most.

4. Encourage your child to become involved in social activities. Where appropriate, go along so you can observe and encourage them to use age-appropriate social skills. Practice one or two of these skills prior to heading out so that the steps are fresh in your child's mind.

5. Make sure that your child has support with daily activities such as school work and social interactions. Pair your child with a tutor, mentor, or another positive role model to provide an encouraging example for your child's maturity to grow.

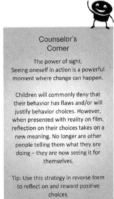

Counselor's Corner

The power of sight. Seeing oneself in action is a powerful moment where change can happen.

Children will commonly deny that their behavior has flaws and/or will justify behavior choices. However, when presented with reality on film, reflection on their choices takes on a new meaning. No longer are other people telling them what they are doing – they are now seeing it for themselves.

Tip: Use this strategy in reverse form to reflect on and reward positive choices.

6. Role-play appropriate social behaviors with your child. You cannot expect them to perform appropriately unless they have been given proper teaching and modeling.

7. Be specific in identifying what social behaviors need to change. Be specific in how your child is to make changes. Practice, practice, practice.

8. Take pictures or video of your child acting in appropriate ways during role-playing. Encourage them to reference

these tools in order to mirror developmentally appropriate behavior.

9. Discuss your observations of your child's behavior with them. Never ask why they act in an immature way. Instead, ask how they feel about their behavior and then work together to create a plan to further develop skills.

10. Teach problem-solving and self-advocacy skills. They will need these skills to effectively counter peer criticisms and social problems.

11. Communicate your concerns and interventions with your child's teacher(s). Tell them what you are working on and what they can do to further support that work. You may even be able to request that your child join a social skills group during school hours.

12. Remember that social skill development in children who are socially behind will take time. Keep practicing and be patient. Your child is blessed to have you working hard on teaching them how to build their social skills.

13. Do not expect that your child will immediately pick up on how to interact socially. There are many social etiquette factors to take into consideration. It is common for children to need repetition before any skill is truly mastered. Take it one step and one skill at a time.

14. Use plenty of positive consequences to reinforce appropriate behaviors. Follow through on these rewards and acknowledgements each and every time. See the "Must-Know Parenting Strategies" chapter and appendix A for further guidance.

15. Do not compare your child to other children. This will only make them feel poorly about themselves. You can however ask them to watch other children their age and then tell you what they see them doing. You can use these observations as starting points in practicing social skills with your child.

16. If you need to correct your child's behavior, do it privately. You do not want to embarrass them in front of others. This may prompt others to pick on your child, exclude them, and/or deflate their self-esteem. Private discussions and practice are best.

17. Establish a code word to use when around others. Use it to secretly remind your child about appropriate interaction skills. Perhaps the secret word will be an indicator that they need to calm themselves. Perhaps it will be to remind them to share. Your child's greatest need or behavioral goal should be what is attached to the code word.

18. Acknowledge other children in your home who are displaying developmentally appropriate skills. Speak specifically on what you saw them do and why those actions make your proud. The immature child will strive to receive some of the positive recognition too by working to further improve their skills. Acknowledge their efforts at your every chance so they get some of your praise too.

19. Ignore immature behavior, such as whining or crying, when it is being used in an attempt to get your child's own way. Tell them that they can discuss what they want when the whining or crying stops.

20. Ignore immature behavior when it is being used in an attempt to gain your attention. Tell them that you will speak and interact with them once they stop [insert behavior] and sit calmly. You then walk away until your child complies.

21. Visit behaviorcorner.com for more information and contact options for getting additional guidance from a professional therapist.

Obsessive-Compulsive Disorder

Introduction

Obsessive-compulsive disorder (OCD) is highly linked with impairment of daily life functioning. Symptoms can come and go in severity over time and may be severe, moderate, or mild. They may fluctuate in their intensity from day to day and week to week. Some common symptoms to look for in children may include

- concern over harm occurring to a loved one;
- concern over germs;
- concern over being dirty;
- checking and rechecking items;
- desire to do things perfectly and becoming upset if perfect is not achieved;
- erasing again and again to get their school work to meet their standards, sometimes to the point of the paper having a hole in it;
- organizing and reorganizing materials at school and belongings at home;
- being very particular about the feeling of their clothing on their skin; and
- needing to equal out body movements (if one hand touches something, the other one has to as well).

OCD can be broken into two parts of understanding. One is defining an obsession. The other is defining a compulsion. When you put these two definitions together, you can gain an understanding of what your child is struggling with.

Formal Diagnosis

According to the American Psychiatric Association, obsessions are defined as thus:

Common Co-Existing Conditions

- Depression
- Low self-esteem
- Anger
- Social deficits
- Anxiety disorders
- Bipolar disorder
- Obsessive-compulsive personality disorder
- Tic disorder
- Attention-deficit/hyperactivity disorder
- Oppositional defiant disorder
- Hair pulling or skin picking

- Repeated and continuous thoughts, urges, or images that are intrusive and unwanted. They cause anxiety or distress in most people.
- The person attempts to ignore or hold back such thoughts, urges, or images, or tries to replace them with some other thought or action through a compulsion.

Compulsions are defined as thus:

- Repetitive behaviors (hand-washing, checking) or mental acts (counting, repeating words or phrases to oneself) that a person feels driven to perform in response to an obsession or according to rules that must be applied perfectly.
- The behaviors or mental acts are used in an attempt to prevent or reduce anxiety or distress or to prevent some dreaded event or situation from happening. However, these behaviors or acts are not realistically linked with what they are designed to prevent or reduce.
- Tip: Young children may not be able to speak about the goals of their behaviors or acts.

The American Psychiatric Association goes on to say that obsessions and compulsions cause daily distress, are time-consuming (take more than one hour a day), or significantly impact a person's daily life and functioning. Lastly, the criteria of OCD must not be better explained by another mental disorder, medical condition, or substance use.

A person living with OCD attempts to remain in control by performing tasks to reassure themselves that everything will be okay and to feel calm. For example, a person may have to check and recheck to make sure the stove knobs are completely straight and in the off position in order to feel secure enough that the house will not burn down. The number of times needed to check the stove may always be a predetermined number or may increase as it takes more reassurance to decrease the anxiety.

Many people describe obsessive-compulsive disorder as feeling "stuck." Their attempts to take control of the situation only result in being ruled by the disorder. With the right help, people can effectively manage their symptoms.

Start using some of these interventions with your child if they are demonstrating the symptoms of obsessive-compulsive disorder:

Interventions

1. Work alongside with your child's pediatrician and with a mental health therapist. These people can best guide you in treating your child from a medical standpoint along with a therapeutic guidance.

2. In order to be a positive and supportive family member, you must deal with your own feelings about your child having OCD. Gain knowledge and support from others in helping you manage your feelings and level of acceptance. None of this is your fault or your child's fault. Your child needs you. You can be their greatest asset in navigating through this diagnosis.

3. Visit the Counselor's Corner at behaviorcorner.com to arrange for online counseling for you and your child.

4. Discuss with your child their feelings about obsessive-compulsive disorder. Ask them how they feel when their OCD symptoms are minimal and how they feel when they

are strong. Does it bother them to feel the way they do? Are they content giving in to the urges? Do they wish they could stop? Each child is different. Gauging how they feel about themselves and the OCD gives a lot of information about the help that they are willing to receive.

5. Educate yourself by joining a support group for parents of children with OCD. Talk with your child's therapist and doctor about needed information for supporting your child. Make peace with not being the expert in this area. There are plenty of people who can help.

6. Be flexible.

7. Put thought into each day and prepare your child for the day's events. Problem-solve any potential struggles. Do not always rearrange things so as to avoid a rough spot for your child. Learning how to adapt and cope is a very useful life skill. Be your child's coach and reward the positive things that come from these trying times.

8. Remember that children with OCD may not be able to move to a new task until they have completed their current activity. Do your best to plan accordingly for this factor.

9. Before a new activity or expectation begins, give your child a few minutes worth of notice so they can prepare for the transition.

10. Whenever possible, give your child notice of a change in routine or schedule.

11. Be prepared to *not* answer your child's questions if they are asking to meet their need for constant reassurance. This need is commonly seen in children with OCD. Although hard, try your best to not answer your child's questions as these answers will only feed the need to keep asking them. Stick to it, and your child will begin to decrease their need to ask for reassurance.

    Tip: You *should* answer your child's everyday questions about life and things that they are curious about.

These answers provide learning experiences and fruitful conversation between the two of you.

Counselor's Corner

Not answering

For those of you who think it is rude to not answer your child, relax! You don't have to be mean about it.

Just simply say, "Asking these questions is not helping you right now. This is my answer, _____. I will not be saying it again. I love you."

12. Always praise your child's positive behaviors.

13. Reward your child's positive choices such as completing their homework, speaking respectfully, helping with the chores, and so on.

14. Maintain routines and a "normal" home environment. Tasks and lives are not to be altered due to this disorder. The more normal the home, the less stress your child will experience.

15. Do not use punishment or physical means as a way to control obsessive-compulsive actions. This will only cause more stress and anxiety. It will also serve to damage your relationship with your child.

   > Stressful situations will increase OCD symptoms

16. Plan for extra time if your child experiences difficulty with transitions and engages in repetitive behaviors. Rushing your child will result in increased stress and anxiety.

17. Acknowledge what makes your child unique apart from their OCD. Children and caregivers can easily get caught up in an OCD life. Obsessive-compulsive disorder is not your child. Your child has many attributes and interests aside from OCD that make them special. Remind them of that and always remind them how much you love them.

18. Talk to your child about how you view their OCD. It is common for children to believe that others in their lives are angry, irritated, or upset with them due to their symptoms. Make it crystal clear that you have only loving feelings toward your child. OCD is something that you will deal with together and will fight for getting better.

19. Never blame your child for their OCD symptoms. OCD is not their fault; if they could stop it they would.

20. Involve your child in activities such as sports, playdates, after-school clubs, and anything else they have an interest in. Having fun is an important part of life and helps us feel our very best.

21. Provide a plan for when your child is not in your care. Communicate with their school, caregivers, relatives, or anyone else supervising your child. Allow them to know about your child's needs and helpful interventions. Special consideration should be given to your child's school day as formal accommodations such as testing or written work modifications may be warranted.

22. Be aware that children who suffer from OCD are at risk for also developing depression, anger, self-esteem issues, and social issues. Seek out the help of a mental health therapist to help effectively deal with these potential issues.

23. Use a journal with your child to identify thoughts and behaviors that they experience on a daily basis. Some of these things will be related to their obsessions, some to their compulsions, and some will be just plain everyday thoughts and actions. Separate these thoughts and actions to help your child further understand how their OCD works and try to make possible plans to help ease their symptoms.

     Hint: It is common for children to hide their compulsions and to deny obsessions. Be observant of your child and have frequent discussions about how you accept their thoughts and actions. Encourage them to be open and honest. Identifying the anxieties and urges are necessary in decreasing the symptoms.

24. Introduce and practice positive self-talk with your child. Positive self-talk is helpful in decreasing obsessions and compulsions. Phrases like "I don't have to listen to you (the intrusive thoughts)" or "I know I will be okay if I don't give in to the urge" can make it easier for your child to refuse the OCD symptoms.

     Always be prepared to support your child in using positive self-talk statements when in the midst of a real obsession and/or compulsion.

Counselor's Corner

Self-Talk 101
The thoughts we think and the words we say highly indicates how we will feel and act when in the midst of a situation.
Negative thoughts of dread, worry, and sadness will likely result in that very experience becoming a reality.
Positive thoughts of "I can do this", "This might be fun", "I am safe", "I know how to get help", "I don't have to do that" and so on allows one to see the security in a situation and gives encouragement.
Positive self-talk is such a powerful tool and anyone can do it. Your child will just need you to show them how.

25. Instill motivation in your child to fight OCD, all the while accepting your child unconditionally and expressing your faith in them to overcome their struggles. This will give them encouragement to strive for independence from OCD.

26. It is okay to admit that you cannot do it all on your own. Getting professional help for your child is not only a good idea, but it is also highly recommended!

27. Visit behaviorcorner.com for more information and contact options for getting additional guidance from a professional therapist.

Pica

Introduction

Pica is an eating disorder and is diagnosed when an individual ingests nonfood items. Diagnosis occurs when the individual is beyond the normal "mouthing" age (twenty-four months) of nonfood items and when at least one month of ingestion causes a negative impact on their daily functioning and health.

Warning signs that a child may have pica include

1. continuous ingesting of nonfood items, even though correction and discouragement has been given; and
2. the child is older than twenty-four months.

Formal Diagnosis

According to the American Psychiatric Association, pica is identified when

- a person continuously eats nonnutritive, nonfood substances over a period of at least one month;
- the eating of nonnutritive, nonfood substances is inappropriate to the developmental level of the person;
- the eating behavior is not considered to be part of a cultural or social practice; and
- if the eating behavior occurs along with another mental disorder, it

Common Co-Existing Conditions

- Medical conditions
- Developmental delays
- Obsessive compulsive disorder
- Autism spectrum disorder
- Intellectual disability
- Schizophrenia
- Hair pulling
- Skin picking

must be severe enough for the person to need additional treatment.

There is not a single reason of what may cause pica to develop. However, researchers have discovered several risk factors for the development of pica. They are as follows:

- Nutritional deficiencies
- One's culture. In some cultures, eating nonfood items is considered normal and accepted.
- Developmental delays or disabilities
- Neglect, little-to-no parental supervision, or limited access to food
- Desire to diet. Some people may try to feel full by ingesting nonfood items.
- Mental health diagnoses such as intellectual disability, autism, and obsessive-compulsive disorder (OCD)
- Pregnancy. Sometimes, pica arises in women during pregnancy and then resolves after birth. In most cases, these women displayed signs of pica as children themselves.

Those with pica frequently crave and ingest nonfood items such as:

Dirt	Clay	Paint chips	Glue
Chalk	Leaves	Erasers	Ice
Baking soda	Coffee grounds	Cigarette ashes	Soap
Burnt match heads	Cigarette butts	Paper towels	Hair
Dust	Buttons	Paper	String
Sand	Toothpaste	Crayons	Feces

Pica can easily result in several grave health concerns. The following are among the most common complications:

- Lead poisoning – can result from ingesting lead-based paint chips
- Intestinal injury – can result if an item punctures or damages the intestine
- Dental injury – can result from chewing hard items
- Infections – can result from eating feces, sand, dirt, and other items containing bacteria
- Anemia–condition concerning red blood cells
- Intestinal problems such as items getting stuck in the intestines or the inability of one's body to eliminate the nonfood item

In some circumstances, immediate action is necessary to protect your child. Examples of this include your child ingesting something poisonous or something harmful.

- If you think your child has ingested something poisonous, immediately call Poison Control at (800) 222-1222.
- If your child has consumed a harmful substance, seek medical care immediately.

> If your child has eaten something poisonous or harmful, get help immediately

Interventions

1. Regardless of your child's age, talk with their doctor. Ingesting nonfood items, whether diagnosed as pica or not, can be very harmful. The doctor will initially run a few tests to determine any health concerns that may be contributing to pica. The tests will be done to also determine if your child is suffering any consequences from ingesting nonfood items such as an infection.

    Your child's doctor is a wonderful resource in helping everyone understand, manage, and prevent pica-related behaviors. Doctors can work with you and your child to provide education on what items are food and which are not. Sometimes hearing this message from a doctor can persuade your child to make food-only choices. Make an appointment today.

2. When struggling with a case of pica that is part of another mental diagnosis, of a developmental delay, or disability, it is extremely important to have ongoing guidance from your child's doctor and from a specialist in the specific area of need that your child has. These two professionals can work with you to develop the best preventative plan for your child.

3. Work with professionals and your child to replace the pica behaviors. Eating nonfood items can easily become a habit that's enjoyable. Everyone needs to use positive supports, behavior planning, supervision, and consistency to help stop the pica behaviors.

4. Visit the Counselor's Corner at behaviorcorner.com to arrange for online counseling for you and your child.

5. The most effective treatment comes from the collaboration between families, medical doctors, specialists, and mental health professionals. Work with these people to create and use a plan in your home to positively support food-only choices. Frequently report back to these professionals on how things are going and if there has been any improvement.

Tip: Some interventions seem as though they can be implemented on your own without a professional's help, and perhaps they can. However, children who are having difficulties typically respond to behavior planning better when working with people who are not part of

Counselor's Corner

Inform the doctor

Although it is a fact that most cases of eating nonfood items resolve on their own, don't wait to let your child's doctor know what has been happening.

So many dangerous things can result from even just experimental ingestion of items.

Be safe and get help.

their family. Don't take it personally; my kids did the same thing. It is completely normal.

6. Be patient. The vast majority of pica cases resolve all on their own. With your support and guidance, your child will more than likely grow out of their pica behaviors.

7. Frequently reward your child for not engaging in pica behaviors. Frequently praise and reward for eating only food.

    When positive reinforcement is given prior to pica behaviors occurring, it is an even stronger reinforcer in discouraging this behavior. Do this multiple times a day and always before your child attempts to eat non-food items.

8. Each time your child attempts to eat a nonfood item, remove it from their hands and replace it with food. Use healthy foods to encourage healthy eating.

9. Use preventative measures in your home. Install child locks and put nonfood items that your child typically ingests out of reach or completely out of your home. Request that all other caregivers do the same.

10. Make an appointment with your child's dentist. Inform the dentist of the struggles that your child is having and ask them to conduct an examination to see if there has been any damage done to your child's teeth. This is another great professional to have in your corner.

11. Always provide supervision. Young children (up to two years) normally explore their surroundings and put things in their mouth. This is a normal part of development and is not considered pica. It is wise to begin discouraging children from mouthing items as they approach the age of two. Continue teaching the difference between food and nonfood items as they grow.

> True cases of pica occur when a child is two or more years of age and continues to eat nonfood items despite being taught otherwise.

12. Remember that patience is key in treating pica because it can take time for some kids to stop wanting to eat non-food items. Consistently use these positive behavior interventions and involve outside professionals to assist your child in overcoming pica.

13. Visit behaviorcorner.com for more information and contact options for getting additional guidance from a professional therapist.

Sensory Processing Concerns

Introduction

Although not included in the Diagnostic and Statistical Manual of Mental Disorders, sensory processing disorder is viewed by many as having a significant impact on children's ability to function.

Experiencing difficulty with processing, organizing, and reacting to sensory input (sound, taste, sight, touch, smell, and others) are among the main concerns with sensory processing disorder.

For the majority of us, our senses work silently and flawlessly to process our surroundings. Imagine for a minute that you are having difficulty with balance, overwhelmed by smells, or sensitive to what touches your skin every single day (these are only a few of examples); while those around you seem to manage the same environmental input with ease. Do you think you would struggle with that? Would you want help? Of course, the answer to both of those questions would be yes.

Symptoms of sensory processing disorder may present very differently from person to person. Those with sensory processing disorder may experience sensory symptoms ranging from mild to severe and may be effected in anywhere from one sense to many senses. Just as in all aspects in life, individuals are unique, and those with sensory processing concerns will present with various symptoms.

Common Co-Existing Conditions

- Attention-deficit/hyperactivity disorder
- Poor social skills
- Anxiety
- Depression
- Behavior difficulties
- Autistic spectrum disorder
- Learning deficits
- Self-esteem concerns

Although your child's sensory needs are very important, they may not be the only area of concern. Those who have sensory processing deficits may also suffer from behavior problems, anxiety, depression, social exclusion, and/or perform poorly in school. It is important to have your child screened for sensory issues if they struggle in any of those areas.

Keep in mind that misdiagnosis is common given that many sensory concerns mirror those behaviors frequently found in other childhood disorders such as ADHD, autism spectrum disorder, anxiety, learning disorders, obsessive compulsive disorder, and more.

To find a provider who is experienced in treating sensory processing disorder visit the Sensory Processing Disorder Foundation at www.spdfoundation.net

This foundation's website provides you with accurate information and gives support for those who have children with sensory needs. One of the great resources that they offer is the sensory processing disorder symptom checklist broken down by age. Although no checklist can diagnose or take the place of a professional's care, it can give parents valuable insight into symptoms that their child is displaying.

Formal Diagnosis

Sensory processing disorder does not exist as a formal diagnosis from the American Psychiatric Association. Nonetheless, it is a real condition that affects many children and adults.

Interventions

1. Work with an occupational therapist who has knowledge and experience in using a sensory integration approach. You can find a professional experienced in this area by using the directory found at www.spdfoundation.net

2. Contact your child's doctor to consult about your child's sensory needs. A medical professional is a key person that will help in the treatment process.

3. Visit the Counselor's Corner at behaviorcorner.com to arrange for online counseling for you and your child.

> Treatment strategies work best when
> they are used during treatment
> and regularly in the home.

4. Put what you learn to use at home. Attending occupational therapy with your child is a wonderful step in the
right direction. However, effective treatment for your
child will not occur during weekly sessions alone. It will
occur when the sensory integration techniques learned in
session are used at home throughout each and every day.

   It is expected that a child being treated for sensory
concerns will have a sensory diet that gives them input,
exercises, space, and whatever else they need to cope in
all areas of their day. Your child's needs do not stop when
you leave treatment.

5. Have patience. A lot of planning goes into helping a child
with sensory processing disorder. Plan your child's sensory
diet each day and plan for ways to use this diet in order to
be preventative during the daily routine.

6. You must communicate your child's needs to school staff
and to other providers. Sign a release of information so
that your child's occupational therapist and other providers can speak with your child's school and with each
other. Ensuring that your child is receiving services and
their sensory diet needs when out of your care is critical
for success.

7. Prepare your child ahead of time for transitions. Expecting
your child to immediately respond to your request to stop
a current task and to start something new will likely cause
a battle. Set a visual timer five to ten minutes prior to
the transition. Also, provide verbal reminders of the time
remaining every few minutes. If your child continues
to struggle with transitions, you may need to role-play
this skill.

8. Limit the amount of visuals on the ceiling and walls in your home. Request that the same be done in other caregiver's homes and in your child's classroom. Too much can cause visual overload!

9. Organize your child's toys, school supplies, and other commonly used items into bins labeled with the name of the item(s) along with a picture. This helps your child find things easier without becoming overwhelmed. Everyone will appreciate this intervention.

10. With your child, draw a map showing where everything in their room belongs to help them visualize where to put their belongings.

11. Post visual reminders of the skills that are currently being working on. This could be placed on the bathroom mirror, on the back of your car seat so they see it while riding, or on the fridge.

Counselor's Corner

Posting skills

An intervention is always implemented a bit easier when examples are given. So here you go...when deciding to post visual reminders of the skills that your children are working on give these a gander:

1. Academic skills may include spelling words or math facts.
2. Social skills may include smiling at others or writing an example of how to use words to solve a problem.
3. A behavior skill could be listening to mom and dad the first time.

Whatever skill you and your children are working on, having a visual reminder in various places for them to see will help to reinforce their new skill sets.

12. Prepare your child to the best of your ability for changes in routine.

13. Provide earplugs and give warnings of anticipated loud noises such as fireworks, an announcement in the grocery store, or loud sounds at an amusement park. Depending on the severity of your child's sensory issues, these may

not be places that your child can attend until adequate treatment and growth has been established.

14. Provide physical sensory input. Gently roll a large, light-weight ball on your child while they are lying down; provide them with a weighted blanket or vest; and/or rub areas of their body such as back, arms, or head to promote calming.

15. Provide a quiet, safe place for your child to go when they feel overstimulated. You may need to direct your child there until they get old enough to independently identify when their body and brain need this time away.

16. Allow your child to stand, sit on a ball, chew gum, lie in a bean bag chair, have handheld manipulatives or whatever else is needed while speaking with you or while completing tasks. Share these ideas with those who care for your child for when you are not around.

> Meeting one's sensory needs
> promotes better decision-making.

17. Remember, sensory processing disorder presents differently in people. Try many options and listen to your child when they tell you (or their behavior tells you) what they need to manage the sensory input being received. Providing for your child's needs will reduce the chance of experiencing sensory overload.

18. Do not use fluorescent lighting. These lights send out a humming sound that may be distracting and annoying to a child who has heightened hearing. Natural or traditional soft light is best.

19. If your child is sensitive to smells, request that those working with your child do not use strong-smelling scents.

20. At home, be aware of the scent you and others wear. In addition, the scent of the laundry soap, candles, or air fresheners can all be triggers for sensory issues.

21. Don't force your child to eat certain food. Children with sensory needs commonly have difficulty with food textures or tastes. Forcing a child to eat something that is unappealing will only serve to increase your child's resistance to food. You may want to try an incentive program that builds in rewards for trying new foods but not necessarily eating the entire portion.

22. Observe social interactions closely and encourage your child to practice proper social skills. Also, monitor how others interact with your child so as to prevent teasing or bullying due to underdeveloped skills.

23. Practice nonverbal communication with your child. It is helpful to use magazine clippings to visually see facial expressions. Speak about facial characteristics, the feeling(s) the person in the picture may have, and possible reasons for those feelings. Some children who have sensory concerns are not good at picking up on visual cues or facial expressions. Education in this area is important.

24. Work with your child to have clothes that feel as though they fit properly and feel comfortable. This may mean you have five of the same pair of pants. However, your willingness to accommodate your child's sensory needs will save

Counselor's Corner

The fit is everything
Just because clothing technically fits your child. Their sensory needs may disagree. Follow your child's wishes for what feels right and what doesn't.

both of you time and aggravation. Tags on clothing may cause another issue for your child. Choose clothes that have no tags to avoid this annoyance altogether.

25. Be patient and flexible. Show your child how much you love them by meeting their sensory needs and requests whenever possible.

26. Provide a touch-screen computer or tablet when at home and in school to complete computer-generated tasks. Touch screens are easier to use and understand than the traditional personal computers that have a right-and-left-click mouse.

27. When needing to concentrate on a task, provide your child with earplugs to minimize the amount of distracting noise. For some children, listening to quiet and soothing music through headphones works to increase their ability to focus.

28. Provide your child with plenty of exercise and physical activity options. Promote this by providing a trampoline, dancing to music, and doing push-ups with them. All of these examples provide a physical outlet for sensory needs. Hint: Do push-ups against a wall to make this activity more fun. Your child simply leans into the wall with their hands firmly placed and does a standing push-up.

29. Ask your child to be a helper. Carrying a laundry basket, putting away the dishes, sweeping, and washing the car are only a few examples of how sensory needs can be met during the regular routine of the day.

30. Visit behaviorcorner.com for more information and contact options for getting additional guidance from a professional therapist.

Tantrums

Introduction

A child's tantrum can take any challenging parenting situation from bad to worse very quickly. Throwing tantrums is a way that children try to assert control and get their own way. A flood of emotions as they become upset can erupt into one ugly scene.

Tantrums can cost a parent greatly. Sacrifices as a parent happen all the time, some we give joyfully and some we give with much resistance. When a child throws a tantrum and ends up changing our plans, it can cause anyone to want an easy fix.

> Tantrums can be embarrassing and frustrating. Will you survive? Yes! If you strive for long-term solutions.

If you want it fixed right, you must put the time in. Fix it for the long-term, and your rewards will be great. Stop the tantrum for the short-term, and your battles will drag on and on and on.

What will you do?

Being at home when your child pulls this behavior is one thing, but what if you are in public? Will you give in to their demands? Will you survive the embarrassment and frustration?

Simply stated, "Yes, you will survive." The interventions listed here will show you how.

Formal Diagnosis

There is no formal diagnosis for tantrums alone. Although diagnoses exist with tantrums as a symptom, no diagnosis addresses tantrums as the sole symptom.

Interventions

1. Contact your child's doctor and arrange for family counseling from a mental health professional. These two professionals can work with you to identify your child's behavioral needs by ruling out other possible disorders and causes.

   Additionally, using the following interventions under the guidance of a mental health provider will make them even more effective and will help you to stay on track.

2. Visit the Counselor's Corner at behaviorcorner.com to arrange for online counseling for you and your child.

3. Do *not* ever give into your child's behavior by giving them what they want. If you do, you have just taught your child that throwing a tantrum is effective in getting their way. This will guarantee that you will see more tantrums in the future.

   Hint: You must be consistent with this every time

4. When home, direct your child to the time-out place and walk away. If it is not possible to get them to time-out, walk away from where they currently are. Make a statement that when they stop [insert behavior], you will talk about what they want. Be prepared to repeat this more than once. Besides this statement, nothing else should be said unless your child is displaying dangerous behavior.

5. When in public, be prepared to leave with your child. Do this by simply stating, "This behavior is not okay. We are leaving." If your child won't go, you may need to carry him/her.

   Even if this means that you ditch a cart of groceries, do it. The easy road in this situation is to give in to your child's demands so that you can finish the shopping, but what do you think is going to happen the next time you go out? Yup, another behavior display to get what they want. Pay now or pay later—big time. Your choice.

Avoid this mistake. Tell your child that they will get something for leaving nice. If you have decided to leave a place due to inappropriate behavior, don't offer your child something for leaving. This will only teach them that if they misbehave, they will get something out of it eventually.

6. Record your child's tantrum. When they are calm, watch it or listen to it together. Ask your child their opinion. Ask if they feel proud, and if they would want others to see/hear them acting that way. Use their responses as the basis for a behavior plan.

7. Provide many opportunities for your child to experience success throughout the day. When they do, give them plenty of praise. Kids feel good when they are successful and will experience less of a need to have a tantrum when things are going well for them.

8. Once your child is completely calm, talk to them about what their choices are when faced with a similar situation in the future. Be prepared to talk about coping with strong feelings and how to make positive choices.

9. Create a written and visual behavior plan that includes the coping skills and positive choices that were identified during your talk. Do this together and allow them to decorate the plan and to include their opinions. Be sure to include positive and negative consequences that they will earn based on their behavior choices. Use the plan consistently!

10. Teach your child how to use coping skills and positive decision-making. Practice with them through role-playing. This will help your child to feel more confident when faced with strong feelings and tough situations in the future.

Counselor's Corner

Role play to the rescue.

Role play is code for practice. Acting out situations is fun and increases the learning experience for your children. Here are some scenarios that may be helpful to act out when it comes time to practice with them:

1. Mom says that it is time for dinner, but you are on the last level of your game. What are some choices you have to keep calm and to solve the problem?
2. The rule is no snacks before dinner, but you got caught eating cookies. If you could redo your choice, you would.....
3. Mom said that you can ride your bike after dinner, but it started to rain so now you can't. What can you do to stay calm?

11. Regularly praise and reward your child for making positive choices, especially when they feel upset by a situation. Letting them know that you are proud of their actions will give them added motivation to succeed.

12. Give praise and rewards to other children who are in the home when they choose to handle a situation without using a tantrum. Recognize them for specific things that they did right. Your child's desire to get that same praise will increase and so will their desire to stop the tantrums.

13. Communicate with your child's teacher(s) on the struggles that you are seeing at home and inquire into any behavioral concerns occurring during the school day. If needed, work with the teacher to create a behavior plan for the school day that compliments what you are doing at home to promote positive behavior choices.

14. When you are away from your child, all caregivers need to uphold the behavior plan being used at home. Insist that they do not give in your child's wishes if they tantrum.

Instruct all of your child's caregivers to NOT give into your child's wishes if they tantrum

15. Be an example by using coping skills and positive decision-making yourself. Everyone has tough days and strong emotions. When you are experiencing a rough patch, remember that your children are always watching what you do and what you say. You want them to act in a certain way. Showing them how starts with you.

16. Tantrums are common and expected from young children. Consider your child's age and developmental level before requiring that the tantrums stop.

17. Prior to an activity where tantrums have been experienced in the past, remind your child of the expectations such as the use of identified coping skills, communication skills, and problem-solving skills.

18. Prepare your child prior to all activities of what the boundaries and expectations are. Regardless if there has been a history of tantrums, it is good practice for any child to have reminders of the expectations of various situations.

Instruct all of your child's caregivers to NOT give into your child's wishes if they tantrum

19. Try to offer an alternative. When you must say no to your child, try to offer a comparable solution so they feel valued yet know they have to respect your decisions. For example, if you tell your child that they can't get candy at the store, offer them candy you have at home after they finish their next meal.

20. Use distraction. When you see signs that your child is headed toward negative feelings or a tantrum, try to talk it out with them. If they are unwilling, engage them in

an activity or a conversation that will distract them from the upsetting stimuli. Encourage them to talk about their negative feelings after the distraction worked.

21. Keep your cool. A child who throws a tantrum can cause feelings such as anxiety, frustration, embarrassment, disbelief, anger, and guilt in a parent. Keeping your cool to make the best decision given the circumstances will help you use the above interventions to the best of your ability.

22. Visit behaviorcorner.com for more information and contact options for getting additional guidance from a professional therapist.

Tic Disorders

Introduction

Tic disorders are diagnoses where children display motor tics (involuntary physical movements) and/or vocal tics (involuntary sounds).

Tics are classified into two categories: simple and complex.

- Simple motor tics are sudden, brief, repetitive movements that involve a limited number of muscle groups, such as eye blinking, eye darting, finger flexing, facial grimacing, shoulder shrugging, sticking the tongue out, and head or shoulder jerking, to name a few.

- Simple vocalizations can include repeated throat-clearing, sniffing/snorting, yelling, hiccupping, grunting sounds, etc.

- Complex motor tics are unique, coordinated patterns of movements that involve more than one muscle group. These can include facial grimacing combined with a head twist and a shoulder shrug, hopping, touching others, gestures, smelling objects, jumping, twisting, and more.

- Complex vocal tics contain words or phrases. A few examples of this include the use of varying tones of voice as

Common Comorbid Conditions

- Attention-deficit/hyperactivity disorder
- Obsessive compulsive disorder
- Anxiety
- Depression
- Bipolar disorder
- Executive functioning deficits
- Medical conditions
- Substance use

one speaks, repeating oneself, or repeating the phrases of others.

Simple tics are normally seen as the beginning signs of a tic disorder. Tics generally start on the head and become more frequent in other areas of one's body over time.

Formal Diagnosis

The American Psychiatric Association describes a tic as a sudden, rapid, recurrent, nonrhythmic motor movement or vocalization. In other words, a tic is an ongoing movement or sound that happens suddenly, quickly and has no set regularity.

There are four types of tic disorders. Each one is listed below and must have onset of symptoms before the age of eighteen.

Tourette's disorder occurs when multiple motor tics are accompanied by one or more vocal tics. The motor and vocal tics do not need to occur at the same time, but they do need to be present at some point during the illness. These tics may come and go, but they need to have continued for more than one year since the first tic started. Lastly, the tics are not due to the effects of substance use or of another medical condition.

Persistent (chronic) motor or vocal tic disorder is diagnosed when single or multiple motor *or* a vocal tic(s) have occurred during the illness—but not both motor and vocal tics. The presenting motor *or* vocal tic(s) may come and go, but they need to have continued for more than one year since the first tic started. Lastly, the tics are not the effects of substance use or of another medical condition, and the person must never have met the criteria for Tourette's disorder.

Provisional tic disorder includes single or multiple motor and/ or vocal tics that have occurred for less than one year since the first tic started. Lastly, the tics are not the effects of substance use or of another medical condition, and the person must never have met the criteria for Tourette's disorder or persistent (chronic) motor or vocal tic disorder.

Other specified tic disorders and unspecified tic disorders may be diagnosed when a person has tics but does not fit the criteria listed above for a tic disorder.

The symptoms of a tic disorder typically start between the ages of five and seven. We see symptoms worsen in adolescents before decreasing and sometimes even resolving into adulthood.

Regardless if tics are diagnosed or undiagnosed, the impact on children's functioning is typically negative. They tend to struggle with peer relationships, emotional development, and socialization. In some cases, these children also struggle with showing appropriate behaviors and do best with low stress levels in order to avoid becoming overwhelmed.

Your child deserves support and unconditional understanding. These interventions work to give them exactly that!

Interventions

1. Work with your child's doctor and a mental health professional to develop a treatment plan to help your child cope. Therapy and coping includes much more than dealing with just the tics. It should address the resulting effects that a tic disorder can have on a child. Some of these include sleep disturbances, low self-esteem, self-consciousness of how others view them, depression, aggression, impulsivity, and the need for relaxation techniques.
    These concerns along with the tics themselves could potentially be reduced in number with effective treatments.
2. Visit the Counselor's Corner at behaviorcorner.com to arrange for online counseling for you and your child.
3. Be patient as the process of managing tics needs to be viewed in terms of years, not months. The presence of tics in Tourette's syndrome and chronic tic disorder may last a lifetime.

4. Find a child-based group or center that runs activities or group counseling for those with a tic disorder. Being around others who have tics and who truly understand help to make your child feel less alone and more accepted.

5. Find a support group for yourself and for your family to attend. Frequently, there are supportive activities for family members that go along with the groups that you find for your child to participate in.

6. In order to be a positive and supportive family member, you must deal with your own feelings about your child having a tic disorder. Gain knowledge and support from others in helping to manage your feelings and level of acceptance. None of this is your fault or your child's fault. Your child needs you. You can be their greatest asset in navigating through this diagnosis.

7. Remember, tics are not done by choice. They are involuntary, which means your child cannot control them for long periods of time.

8. Never blame your child for a tic.

9. Do not use positive or negative consequences in an attempt to control tic behaviors. Children who have a tic disorder often have behaviors that come and go and with varying intensity. They also demonstrate a large range of abilities in being able to control their tic behaviors.

10. To address unacceptable behavior, role-play desirable behaviors. This allows for a teaching approach rather than a punishment approach. This is very important!

11. Keep teaching, practicing, and reteaching social skills and acceptable behaviors that occur outside of the tics themselves.

12. Provide consistent routines and structure.

13. Allow your child to take breaks from activities to go to a private place to release tics if they choose.

14. Plan ahead by discussing the day's schedule with your child. Be sure to include some flexibility time to account

for the unseen factors of the day. This will help to make them feel prepared and confident.

15. Keep your child up-to-date on any changes in routine when possible. Sudden changes can result in a decrease of behavior control and an increase in anxiety.

16. Speak with your child's teacher(s) about their needs and put a plan in place for managing and reacting to the tics. Some things to request of the teaching staff may include

- your child teaching their classmates about their needs and diagnosis, if they are comfortable in doing so;
- allowing for movement breaks and a private area to get the tics out, especially if your child tends to suppress them;
- appropriate responses for the adults and students to make in response to tics;
- establishing a system for your child to communicate their needs to the teacher;
- the use of a computer to complete written work if fine motor skills are impacted; and
- extra time to complete assignments and tests.

17. Gain a neuropsychological evaluation of your child's strengths and needs. Be prepared to attend several meetings until the evaluation is complete. This is especially true with children who have a tic disorder because they may decide to suppress the tics until done with the appointment. Use the evaluation results to create a supportive plan for home and school.

18. Work with your child to improve social skills and self-esteem if needed. (Appendix B and appendix C have activities for improving one's self-esteem and assertiveness skills.) These are key factors in helping to manage tic behaviors.

19. Do not allow your child to become overly stimulated. This could cause them to lose control of their behavior.

20. Provide a safe, quite place for your child to regain calmness. This quiet place is not to be used for punishment. On the contrary, the independent use of this safe place can result in building personal power and responsibility.

21. Agree on a nonverbal signal that your child can use to notify you when they need to spend time in the quiet place. This could be a time-out signal given with their hands or a note that simply says "quiet place."

> Be patient.
> Although tics can be suppressed for a time, they are not done by choice.
> A tic disorder may last a lifetime.

22. Surround your child with positive role models. These people (yourself included) need to be willing to use coping skills to keep frustrations and anxieties under control. When your child sees how you handle various situations, they will follow your example.

23. Plan for plenty of physical activity. Exercise helps to relieve stress and assists in our brain's processing of information more efficiently.

24. Provide your child with adult supervision especially during stressful times. Knowing that you or another trusted adult is close by will help to ease possible anxiety. Children with tics typically feel more comfortable interacting with adults over peers.

25. Give frequent positive praise and build your child's self-esteem by pointing out and promoting all the wonderful traits and behaviors they possess.

26. Be flexible and willing to adjust to your child's behavior and needs. Your support and patience is of the utmost importance.

27. Regularly teach and practice appropriate responses to various life events. Knowing how to solve a problem will help to reduce anxious thoughts, instill confidence in your child, and result in fewer tics. Being prepared goes a long way!

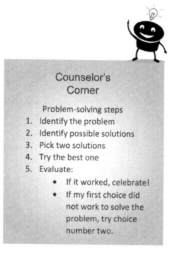

Counselor's
Corner

Problem-solving steps
1. Identify the problem
2. Identify possible solutions
3. Pick two solutions
4. Try the best one
5. Evaluate:
   - If it worked, celebrate!
   - If my first choice did not work to solve the problem, try choice number two.

28. Structure your child's environment to prevent high anxiety and stress. Ensure that they have plenty of supports and coping options available if needed. This includes at home, in school, at relatives' homes, or anywhere else your child spends time.
29. For Tourette's disorder patients, visit the National Tourette Syndrome Association at tsa-usa.org
30. Visit behaviorcorner.com for more information and contact options for getting additional guidance from a professional therapist.

Unmotivated

Introduction

Control, control, control. This is what you can look toward as a likely reason for a child's lack of motivation. Sometimes children are searching for consistency and control in their lives. This could be due to a sudden change such as a parent's divorce, the birth of a sibling, a move, or violence at home. These life upheavals cause children to seek out any form of control they can get. This includes the area of motivation.

Your child makes their own choices; they choose to be motivated or unmotivated. Your job is to encourage them to show motivation by meeting their needs for consistency, safety, and appropriate control.

It is common for a lack of motivation to continue as children grow, unless there are people who are willing to help reverse these unmotivated characteristics.

A second possibility that may cause a child to show signs of lack of motivation has to do with the amount of responsibility and level of expectations set for them. If caregivers do everything for a child and don't expect them to have any accountability or responsibility, the child isn't given a reason to be motivated to complete tasks. On the flip side, if expectations are set too high, the child will feel helpless to succeed, which results in them not attempting tasks at all. To find the magic combination of responsibility and expectations for your child, take into consideration their abilities and age.

Another possible cause for a child to appear unmotivated is lack of knowledge. If one does not know how to complete a task or even how to start, behaviors such as avoidance and lack of motivation may appear.

If you haven't guessed it yet, it isn't just your child who has to make some changes. You do too! Read on to figure out what you can do to master this most important job.

Formal Diagnosis

There is no formal diagnosis for one who is unmotivated alone. Although diagnoses exist with lack of motivation as a symptom, no diagnosis addresses one being unmotivated as the sole symptom.

Interventions

1. Consult with your child's doctor and a mental health professional about your concerns. Lack of motivation could be a symptom of a medical or mental disorder that requires attention. Consulting with these two professionals will help to identify your child's individual needs.
2. Visit the Counselor's Corner at behaviorcorner.com to arrange for online counseling for you and your child.
3. Sign your child up for extracurricular activities. This could include after-school clubs or community events.
4. Frequently spend one-on-one time with your child. Pick an activity that they will enjoy such as watching a movie, creating a craft, going for a bike ride, playing video games, and so on.
5. Give extra help in school or at home to support your child in completing tasks. Many times, children's interest in a task will increase through the support of a behavior plan. When feeling as though an activity is important, interesting, and challenging, children (and adults) are more likely to engage. Spend some time talking with your child about what they feel would help to motivate them.
6. Tell and show your child what you expect. Ensure that they have adequate ability and understanding to meet your

expectations. Give plenty of time to practice and always be a positive role model. Your high level of engagement in meeting the daily expectations will be a good example for your child.

7. Provide a calm and safe home environment to foster a sense of security. This will promote a decreased need for additional control behaviors.

8. Teach problem-solving skills. A child who has healthy ways to cope and who can take positive steps to solve dilemmas is able to navigate through life's difficulties without resorting to destructive behaviors. Teaching and reteaching will be necessary to make sure these skills are well learned.

9. Give your child independence to get things done on their own. This is a healthy way to hand over some control to your child. The best way to do this is to work together to create a list of what their responsibilities are. Post the list in clear sight as a reminder of the tasks.
   Tip: Put their ideas on the chart too—after all if you have 100 percent control of what goes on the list, your child will likely resist this activity too.

10. Encourage overall wellness. Your child should be getting exercise daily, eating nutritious meals, and getting enough sleep. These are basic needs that we all need to do our best.

11. Identify what motivates and interests your child and use these as incentives for when your child completes tasks and follows your directions. Humans are always motivated to do things their way. If you can use incentives unique to your child, you can encourage them to achieve the results that they (and you) are looking for.

   Tip: Identify incentive choices with your child and establish them prior to giving your child a task. If you wait until your child displays avoidance before offering the incentive, you end up teaching them that their avoidance has a payoff.

12. Give your child control over some personal and family decisions so they begin to feel as though they can let go of some of the inappropriate controlling behaviors.

13. Create a feelings box with your child. This is a private box where your child can store their feelings and thoughts. These feelings and thoughts can be put into written words or drawings. With your child, arrange a time each day that you will look in the box with or without them. This can be a very good way for the two of you to communicate in a nonthreatening way.

14. Foster your child's strengths and interests by pointing out what makes you proud. Do this by using your words and by leaving notes around the house for them to find.

15. Make it fun. Encourage your child to use their imagination as they are completing a task. Tell them to think of the task as a game; when they finish the task they win the game and get to celebrate.

16. Practice relaxation techniques with your child especially before a difficult task. Having a relaxed mind makes it easier to start a task versus being in a stressed-out state.

17. Provide consequences. For example, if your child doesn't do their chores and homework, they are not allowed to participate in television and video game time. They will

be expected to do the chores and homework first. This needs to be a preestablished consequences for all children in the home. Following through on consequences teaches your child an important lesson about being responsible for their own actions.

18. Remain calm. Getting upset will not help increase your child's motivation. In fact, it may make it worse.

19. Visit behaviorcorner.com for more information and contact options for getting additional guidance from a professional therapist.

Appendix A

Behavior Plans
An Overview

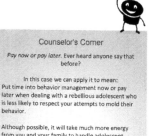

Behavior planning is the cornerstone to changing behavior. Without incentive, there is no motivation.

Incentives can include physical rewards such as toys. Alternately, they can be intangible such as verbal acknowledgements or extra privileges. Incentives can also be internally driven by your children. For example, doing the right thing results in them feeling proud. We call this intrinsic motivation.

Counselor's Corner

Pay now or pay later. Ever heard anyone say that before?

In this case we can apply it to mean: Put time into behavior management now or pay later when dealing with a rebellious adolescent who is less likely to respect your attempts to mold their behavior.

Although possible, it will take much more energy from you and your family to handle adolescent problems instead of supporting your very young children in making positive choices. This support while young is the foundation that your children will use to make positive future decisions.

You get to decide where you are going to devote your life's time and energy. Will you positively support your children to do the right things or will you spend it elsewhere?

This should be a no-brainer because it is you who shapes your children into whom they will become. Step up and do the right thing, today!

Doing the right thing simply because it is right is our ultimate goal when behavior planning. When this magical time occurs, there will no longer be a need to have a formal behavior plan in place. Of course, your children will always do well to receive your praise and will benefit from your life guidance, but behavior planning becomes a thing of the past at this point.

As you move along this journey to behavior plan extinction, you will be able to phase out plans when your children meet their goals consistently. At this point, it may mean using only long-term behavior plans, doing away with a school-based plan, replacing current expectations with other goals, and then eventually ending the behavior plan altogether.

Before we can get to that freeing moment, there is work to be done!

I have met countless people over the years who frown upon incentives being used to get children to behave well. They see these things as bribes and believe that children should automatically behave and respect their elders. I am sorry to report that this is not the case. It takes years of extrinsic incentives (those physical and intangible rewards we just spoke about) to create intrinsic motivation in children.

Think about yourself. Are you motivated by anything extrinsic? I bet you are! Going to work to earn a paycheck, saving money to go on vacation, and exercising to achieve a physically fit body are just a few examples that come to mind.

No one is completely intrinsically motivated. However, as adults we have more control to pick what motivates us than our children have. Do everyone a favor and spend some time with your kids to come up with things that motivate them extrinsically *and* intrinsically. When these motivators are used, the results will be an increase in positive behavior and an understanding of how to get one's needs and wants met independently. That is liberating!

When beginning a behavior plan, you should expect that your child's behavior will increase over the next few weeks before leveling off due to normal testing behaviors. This is because they are researching whether the plan is here to stay and if it will be used consistently. Unless there is a major flaw, stick with it before making any changes. Consistency is what your child needs right now.

Creating an effective behavior plan is about to happen for your family. Be excited and have fun! Know that I am excited right there with you!

Advice from the Counselor!
How to Build and Use an Effective Behavior Plan System

- You may have the best ideas.
- You may have the best behavior plan.
- You may have the best support system to help your children succeed.

However…

If you don't use the following tips, your plan will fail.

These things take dedication on your part, but they are well worth it.

Let's walk through these together:

1. Work with your children to create appropriate rules and expectations. Reflect upon these regularly (daily) with them in order to gauge success and struggles and to identify any areas of needed change.

2. When developing the plan, ask your kids how they think things are currently going. What things are going really well? What things would they like to change? This will give everyone insight on how to build the plan. When you include many of your children's ideas, it will greatly increase their motivation to succeed.

3. Identify the behaviors that are a safety concern or those that cause the most negativity for your child and family. Prioritize these to help you and your children create the rules list.

4. Limit the number of rules expected of your child from four to seven years of age. Younger children should have a lower number than older children. This includes at least one to two "gimmie'" expectations talked about in number 5 below.

5. Incorporate some rules and expectations that are easy for your children to achieve. We call these "gimmies." Having some of these "gimmies" helps your children to see that they can succeed at this plan. This results in increased self-esteem and motivation to meet the rest of the expectations in the behavior plan.

6. Allow your children to decorate the plan with their favorite things, such as pictures of their favorite television characters. This will help to make the plan more intriguing.

7. List and post the rules and expectations. State them positively and clearly. Phrase them in terms of the desirable action that you expect from your children. For example, it can state, "Follow directions the first time asked" and "Complete all of your chores each week."

8. Encourage all your children to participate in the plan. This creates healthy competition and motivation to do their very best.

9. Before holding your children accountable, it is very important to provide examples of how to follow each rule. Use your words to explain what they are to do *and* show your children how to do it through role-playing.

   Tip: It is very useful to change roles and have your children show *you* how to follow the rules. This is a perfect way to ensure that your children have full understanding.

10. Enforce the rules' consistency without fail. Consistency is the foundation that will help your children stay within their boundaries and make positive choices.

11. Work with your children to create a combination of positive rewards (a.k.a. positive consequences) and appropriate negative consequences. These consequences should be aimed at replacing your children's need to misbehave by giving them a similar payoff (attention, power, etc.). Periodically review these consequences with your children and make changes as needed.

   Tip: Use physical tokens such as stickers, play money, chips, etc. to represent earned rewards. Allow your children to turn in these tokens in exchange for the agreed upon positive incentive options.

It is helpful to put the reward options on a menu or list for your children to choose from. Assign each incentive a value. Make some cost only a small amount of tokens, while others should cost much more to teach your children perseverance and responsibility. This method also gives your children more control over the plan by allowing them to choose how to spend their earned tokens versus you telling them what incentive they have earned.

Never take back earned tokens or other positive rewards. Once earned, they cannot be taken away. However, you may restrict the use of your children's tokens until they serve the consequences that result from poor behavior.

> Keep reading for a list of creative, positive rewards to give your child's menu of options a kick start.

12. A bit more on positive consequences: when children can see a positive connection between their behavior plan and an improvement in their behavior, they will be more encouraged to make a lasting change.

13. A bit more on negative consequences: when developing these consequences, ask your children what they think the consequence should be for breaking a rule. Try to compromise, but ultimately, you decide if that idea should be used or not. Make sure the consequence is directly related to the misbehavior for your child to gain the most learning from the experience.

Ensure that the consequences *never* consist of physical punishment such as hitting. This only creates more of a problem along with an ineffective behavior plan.

14. Your children and adult members of your household must be fully aware of the consequences. Adults must use them each time it is necessary.

15. Give your children acknowledgment for effort that they put forth in achieving their goals. Giving partial rewards for this effort will work to teach them that they do not have to be perfect and that you realize the positive steps that are being taken.

16. Be prepared to give your children bonus tokens to reward extra effort that they show. In addition, celebrate these extras with plenty of verbal praise and hugs.

17. When acknowledging your children's effort and successes, be specific in what you observe and what your children have accomplished. Being specific instead of general shows your children that you take a genuine interest in what they do. Putting together a positive behavior system screams this loud and clear!

18. Review your children's successes and shortcomings as soon as possible after they happen. At the very least, reflect upon the day as a whole each night. Develop a tracking sheet to help you do this effectively. This sheet should list each expectation and have a place to mark off when and if it was completed.

19. Behavior plans become even more successful when you and your child's school work together. Create a daily communication tool between your child's teacher(s) and home to reward your child for making positive decisions while at school.

Possible Positive Rewards

It is not necessary to always reward your children with things bought from the store. Although they are powerful rewards, there are alternative options that can be even more powerful.

You may find some of the following ideas a perfect fit for your family. Use these twenty-one ideas to get your creative juices flowing. Don't forget to get your children's input when deciding which rewards to use.

1. Spend alone time with Mom or Dad doing a preferred activity.
2. Call a relative to tell them about good choices made and rewards earned.
3. Have a friend over.
4. Go to a friend's house.
5. Have an extra snack.
6. Watch an extra television show.
7. Make ice cream sundaes.
8. Stay up twenty minutes past bedtime.
9. Earn points or tokens on a point-system behavior plan.
10. Rent a movie or video game.
11. Go to the movie theatre.
12. Have extra outside time.
13. Have Mom or Dad do my chores.
14. Eat a meal different than the family is having.
15. Go on a family bike ride.
16. Choose to eat at a restaurant for a meal.
17. Take a trip to an arcade.
18. Go ice skating or rollerblading.
19. Have a sleepover.
20. Go out for ice cream.
21. Take a trip to the zoo.

Quick and Easy Ways to Improve Behavior

You have endless options and ways to implement ideas that can best meet the needs of your family. The following are just a few ideas to help spark your creativity. Although fun and effective, these in no way compare to the detailed learning and cooperation that is found when using the behavior plan system described above.

1. Create a rules box where the household rules are written on pieces of paper. Every time your children follow a rule, they can take the corresponding paper and put it a container. Once the container is full, a reward is given.
    Tip: If you give each child their own container, each of your children will want to be first to fill theirs. This quickly changes misbehavior to dazzling decision-making. Jackpot!

2. Work with your child to identify several items or privileges that they want. Write each one down on a separate piece of paper and place each piece of paper in identical envelopes. Each time your child does not follow a rule within one warning, one envelope is taken away.
    At the end of the day, your child is able to pick from the remaining envelops to see what has been earned.

3. If you have a child who struggles to communicate their feelings, thoughts, needs, or wants, create a plan that has nonverbal ways to communicate. Possible ideas include the following:

    *   Index cards that have a word written on it or a picture to indicate how your child is feeling or thinking. This could be "time-out" or a picture of hands showing the time-out signal if your child is going to their safe place.
    *   Use color-coded cards to help your child tell you how they are feeling. It is helpful to put one feeling picture on each card as well.
    *   Give your child a notebook to write or draw their feelings, thoughts, needs, or wants. At a predetermined time each day, review these with your child. It is best if there

are no other distractions. Your child needs to be heard and know that they have your undivided attention.

• Allow your child to wear a hat or to carry a stuffed animal as a signal that they need to be left alone. Once the hat or stuffed animal is put away, you know that your child is ready to rejoin the family.

Keep the tools you create with your child in a central location so that they can be easily accessed in times of need. If your child cannot find what they are looking for quickly, they will not use them, and you may see an increase in negative behaviors.

Short-Term Behavior Plans

The beauty of short-term behavior plans is that your child is provided with immediate positive reinforcement for a job well done. Begin by identifying one goal per sheet. The goal(s) should address the prioritized expectations that you and your child spoke about when creating the rules and expectations for your home. (See the beginning of this appendix under Advice from the Counselor for a refresher on this topic.)

The example below shows a simple sticker-chart system that has two levels of rewards. The first is receiving an immediate reward in the form of a sticker, check mark, or a smiley face for doing what they are told the first time. The second is an ice cream sundae for filling in all the boxes. Completion of this plan should happen quickly due to the amount of direction normally given to a child in a day.

Based on personal and professional experience, young children do well with this format and become very excited each time they get to place a sticker on their chart. They are being positively reinforced throughout the day and love the attention they get for meeting their goal.

Note: The following page has a blank short-term behavior plan for you to use when creating a personal plan with your child.

Short-Term Behavior Plan Example

Insert child's goal here
(Jonny will do what he is told without reminders)

Insert reward here
(Jonny will get to make his own ice cream sundae for earning a sticker in each box)

Long-Term Behavior Plans

Long-term behavior plans work on the premise that the child using it has the ability to meet the goal without continuous reinforcement given. Generally, small steps are taken to obtain a large reward.

In the example below, the child is working to meet an identified goal for a solid week in order to earn a video game rental. During the week, there are daily check-ins. Once all checks are earned, the reward is given.

If you choose to use a long-term behavior plan, you must check in with your child daily to reflect upon how things are going. It is most effective to praise or to give redirection on the day (or in the moment) it occurred. Remembering what happened two days is ago is hard to do and ineffective in teaching your child.

Spend time daily to make the plan most effective.

Note: The following page has a blank long-term behavior plan for you to use when creating a personal plan with your child.

Long-Term Behavior Plan Example

Insert child's goal here
(Jonny will complete his chores without being asked for one week)

Insert reward here
(Jonny will get to rent a video game if he gets a check mark in each box)

Sunday	Monday	Tuesday	Wednesday	Thursday	Friday	Saturday

Sunday	Monday	Tuesday	Wednesday	Thursday	Friday	Saturday

Combined Short- and Long-Term Behavior Plans

You get the best of both worlds when combining short- and long-term behavior plans. Giving positive reinforcement to your child throughout the day all while working toward a larger reward that can be achieved in the future is extremely motivating and fun.

In the example below, Jonny earns a sticker for his chart each time he meets his goal. This is possible to do numerous times a day. Upon filling the chart, the child will earn a puzzle piece. Once all puzzle pieces are put together, the larger reward is earned.

Note: The following page has a blank combined behavior plan for you to use when creating a personal plan with your child.

Combined Short and Long-Term Plan Example

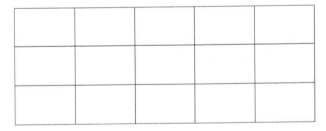

When I earn all of the stickers on my chart, I will get to put a piece to my airplane puzzle together.

When I earn all of the stickers on my chart, I will get to:

_____

_____

_____

Visual Behavior Plans

Easy and *fun* are two words that come to mind when I think of visual behavior plans. These plans are especially useful for children who cannot read or who have a disability that prevents them from understanding the written format of a behavior plan.

In the example below, the child sees what behavior is expected and what reward will be given for successfully meeting the expectation. These rewards need to be given immediately after completion of the task.

Visual Plan Example

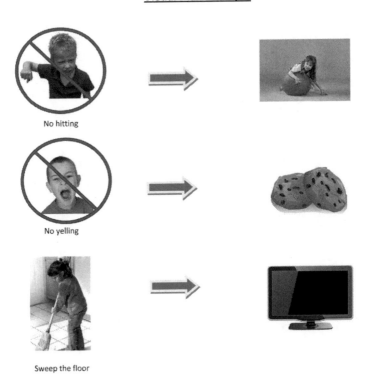

No hitting

No yelling

Sweep the floor

Home-to-School Behavior Plans

Extending home-based behavior plans to school teaches your children that respectful and responsible behavior traits need to be shown in all areas of their day.

Work directly with your child's teacher(s) to establish what type of plan would be manageable to implement and would be effective at the same time. Don't assume that the teacher(s) will just do what you give them. Ask for their input and work together to form the best plan possible.

The examples that follow allow for daily communication to occur between you and teacher(s).

Note: Each example is followed by a blank plan for you and your child to use when creating a plan specific to their needs.

Counselor's Corner

Why is my child acting differently in school?

Attending school is an experience for all of us. The dynamics of school are very different then they are in our homes.

Schools have very structured days.
Students are expected to follow specific rules as they transition from one task to the next. They are very busy during their school day which leaves them with very little time to test the limits.

On countless occasions, parents have struggled to understand why their child is having behavior problems at home but not at school. If you have ever wondered that same thing, no worries – this is very common.

As they should, children feel much more comfortable at home. Home is also less structured. Again, as it should be. Take advantage of this by continuing to teach your child through positive discipline.

Don't be surprised if your child's teachers are unwilling to implement a home-to-school plan when there are no concerns in school. Accept this and praise your child for doing well in school. Perhaps the teachers and you can agree on weekly emails.

Home-to-School Plan Example I

Jonny's Daily Report

Time	Points Earned	Behavior Goals	
8:00-9:00	Initials:	• Following classroom rules • Following directions • Completed assignments • Good peer interactions • Good adult interactions	_____ _____ _____ _____ _____
9:00-10:00	Initials:	• Following classroom rules • Following directions • Completed assignments • Good peer interactions • Good adult interactions	_____ _____ _____ _____ _____
10:00-11:00	Initials:	• Following classroom rules • Following directions • Completed assignments • Good peer interactions • Good adult interactions	_____ _____ _____ _____ _____
11:00-12:00	Initials:	• Following classroom rules • Following directions • Completed assignments • Good peer interactions • Good adult interactions	_____ _____ _____ _____ _____
12:00-1:00	Initials:	• Following classroom rules • Following directions • Completed assignments • Good peer interactions • Good adult interactions	_____ _____ _____ _____ _____
1:00-2:00	Initials:	• Following classroom rules • Following directions • Completed assignments • Good peer interactions • Good adult interactions	_____ _____ _____ _____ _____

Comments:

_____   _____

Teacher's Signature   Parent's Signature

Daily Report

Time	Points Earned	Behavior Goals	
	Initials:	• • • • •	——— ——— ——— ——— ———
	Initials:	• • • • •	——— ——— ——— ——— ———
	Initials:	• • • • •	——— ——— ——— ——— ———
	Initials:	• • • • •	——— ——— ——— ——— ———
	Initials:	• • • • •	——— ——— ——— ——— ———
	Initials:	• • • • •	——— ——— ——— ——— ———

Comments:

Teacher's Signature

Parent's Signature

Home-to-School Plan Example II

NAME: Jonny

DATE:

Goal	Morning Work	Centers	Reading	Writing	Math
I will sit in my seat. If I need to get up, I will raise my hand and ask the teacher.					
I will get ALL of my work done.					

Each time I finish a goal, I will get a sticker on my chart. Mrs. Smith, Mom, and Dad will be very proud of me. If I earn at least 6 stickers a day I will earn 20 points at home.

Comments:

_____
Teacher's Signature

_____
Parent's Signature

NAME:

DATE:

Goal					

Each time I finish a goal, I will get a sticker on my chart. If I earn at least 6 stickers a day I will earn _____.

Comments:

_____   _____
Teacher's Signature   Parent's Signature

Home-to-School Plan Example III

Jonny's Star Sheet

Date:_____

I will earn a star every 30 minutes if I meet my goal.

This sheet will go home with me every day and returned to Mrs. Smith the next morning.

8:30- 9:00	9:00- 9:30	9:30- 10:00	10:00- 10:30	10:30- 11:00	11:00- 11:30	11:30- 12:00	12:00- 12:30	12:30- 1:00	1:00- 1:30	1:30- 2:00

Jonny's goal:

1.   Given no more than 2 teacher reminders, I will follow her direction.

Comments:

_____   _____
Teacher Signature   Parent Signature

Star Sheet

Date:_____

I will earn a star every 30 minutes if I meet my goal.

This sheet will go home with me every day and returned to _____the next morning.

8:30-9:00	9:00-9:30	9:30-10:00	10:00-10:30	10:30-11:00	11:00-11:30	11:30-12:00	12:00-12:30	12:30-1:00	1:00-1:30	1:30-2:00

_____'s goal:

1.

Comments:

_____
Teacher Signature

_____
Parent Signature

Expectations Paired with Rewards

In the following example, you will find three household rules complete with specific ways to accomplish each rule. The examples tell your child exactly what you expect. How great is that? No excuses and no guess work!

Once a task is finished, your child can check the box and earn rewards based on how many tasks were accomplished each day. These rewards should have been selected by you and your child prior to the start of the plan. Remember, children will respond more positively to a behavior plan when they have had a say in its creation.

When looking at the reward section, you will see that there are different levels of reward options available. This is because we are not perfect and neither are your children. They will have rough days. Despite this, it is critical to reward and acknowledge them for what they have done.

A plan of this nature is extremely flexible. Rules can be updated or changed based on the needs of your family and the goals that you all are trying to achieve. Always be willing to take your children's opinions into consideration. The more power they feel they have in the decision-making process, the more powerful the plan will be.

Lastly, review this plan with your family at least once a week. Do so by reviewing successes, discussing the positive impact of your children's choices, and reflecting on any changes that may need to occur.

As long as there is a buy-in to the plan, success will be seen!

Expectations Paired with Rewards Example

Smith House Rules:

1. Do my chores.

   - ☐ Dishes that I used are put in the sink.
   - ☐ Toys and supplies that I used are put away.
   - ☐ The floor of my bedroom has *no* items on it.

2. Do my homework.

   - ☐ My homework is completed at my desk.
   - ☐ My homework is done using my best effort.
   - ☐ My homework is left out for Mom to see.

3. Be respectful to other family members.

   - ☐ Say kind things only.
   - ☐ Share.
   - ☐ Keep my hands to myself.

Rewards:

- When all boxes are checked, I get to select a special snack or any other reward listed below.
- If eight boxes are checked, I get to choose one age-appropriate show that I want to watch or any other reward listed below.
- If seven boxes are checked, I earn ten extra minutes of outside time or any reward listed below.
- If six boxes are checked, I earn a piece of gum.
- If five or fewer boxes are checked, I will earn a hug and plan for how to earn more rewards tomorrow.

Increasing Focus

Many parents are concerned about their child's ability to focus. They speak with teachers, doctors, family members, and counselors about their worries. If you are reading this, perhaps you are one of these parents. For some children, they have a diagnosable condition called attention deficit/hyperactivity disorder. This disorder is best treated with a combination of medication and counseling. In other cases, learning a few tricks to help one focus and building upon social skills can help to improve their overall functioning.

Regardless of which category your feel that your child is in, the following plans can help to support your work in teaching your child to focus. As a reminder, refer to the "Attention, Impulsivity, and Hyperactivity" chapter for the full list of interventions to treat your child's focus struggles.

- Visual plans can help your child to independently recall their tasks. These plans can also be used to help one remember tricks to focusing such as taking breaks, positive self-talk, and using a focusing object. Examples of both plans are included in the following pages.
- Timer tracking can assist your child in increasing their motivation to focus and complete tasks. Record the name of the task, how long the timer was set for, and the actual time it took. Reward your child when they beat their time. Rewards can be given after each task or after a pre-established number of successful trials.
- Wiggle plans can be created to give your child a routine to follow when beginning a task and/or when taking a break. Moving and exercising are two great ways to reestablish focus to tasks. Use this tool to create your child's own wiggle plan with them.

Visual Task Plan

Note: The following page has a blank visual task plan for you to use when creating a personal plan with your child.

My Morning Jobs

☐ I got myself dressed

☐ I brushed my teeth

☐ I brushed my hair

☐ I washed my face

☐ I ate breakfast

☐ I fed the dog

My Afternoon Jobs

☐ I did my homework

☐ I put my school supplies in my backpack for tomorrow

☐ I unloaded and reloaded the dishwasher

☐ I fed the dog

☐ I ate dinner

☐ I took a bath or shower

My Morning Jobs

☐

☐

☐

☐

☐

☐

My Afternoon Jobs

☐

☐

☐

☐

☐

☐

Ways to Help Me Focus

Place a picture of your child taking a break here.

Take a break.

Place a picture of your child doing jumping jacks here.

Do fifteen jumping jacks

Place a picture of your child saying positive phrases here.

Say "I can do this" or "It will be okay."

Place a picture of your child using a focus tool here.

Use a handheld item to squeeze as a reminder to focus

Timer Tracking

Job	Timer is set for	It took me this long	Did I beat the timer?
Finish my math homework	30 minutes	28 minutes	YES!!
Do the dishes	15 minutes	12 minutes	YES!!!
Feed the dog	3 minutes	5 minutes	No
Take a shower	15 minutes	10 minutes	YES!!!

A chart like this one can easily be created by hand or on a computer. Just be sure to use it each time and tell your child that you are recording their time. Having a prearranged incentive attached to beating the timer will help your child succeed.

Wiggle Plan

Wiggle, wiggle, wiggle! My body starts to jiggle!

1. Curl my toes.
2. Stretch my fingers.
3. Take a deep breath and reach to the sky.
4. Do fifteen jumping jacks.
5. Bend over and reach the floor.
6. Do arm circles.
7. Stretch my arms.
8. Stretch my legs.
9. Take another deep breath.
10. Get to work.

Wiggle plans work best when each step is created with your child, practiced, and paired with a picture of them completing the step.

The easiest way to create a wiggle plan is to write each step on a piece of poster board and glue pictures of your child completing each one. Keep the wiggle plan in a consistent place so your child can use it when they need to get their wiggles out.

Appendix B

Coping Skills and Managing Emotions in Positive Ways

Coping with strong feelings and difficult situations is tough for people of all ages, especially children.

Your children are at the time of their lives where they are still learning to manage these circumstances. They learn from watching you and practicing skills to help them cope.

When your children are experiencing strong feelings, try your best to point out all the positives *before* unacceptable behavior occurs. This is one way that will help to encourage your child to see that they can handle their feelings. It also works to build confidence and independence.

The following pages can be printed for you and your child to create a coping book together. This book can be bound by staples or by using a hole punch and threading yarn through the holes to hold it together. Encourage your child to decorate their own cover and the pages throughout to give them more motivation to use their coping book.

All the ideas put in this book should be your child's thoughts. However, you should support your child through this process and gently guide them in the direction of positive thinking and positive actions.

Use all the pages if they fit the given situation. Use only a few if you think that is all that is needed.

For ongoing concerns such as separation anxiety, one copy of this book should be sufficient for repeated use.

For a child who has difficulty coping with a variety of issues that life throws their way, several copies may be needed. One for overall coping skills to refer to again and again, and several others based on your child's need to formulate specific plans.

Clearly, this process demands your patience and flexibility. You've got the tools, so let's get started.

Change and Control

Powerful Positive Self-Talk

There are many situations in life that I CAN change.

Some situations I cannot change. I CAN be okay with this.

Change is a part of life. I CAN remember when change made me happy.

Change is something I CAN accept.

Getting upset will not make things better. I CAN use coping skills.

I CAN remain in control of myself.

I make my own choices. I CAN made a good choice now.

I CAN talk to someone.

I CAN take deep breaths.

I CAN take a break.

I CAN cry.

I CAN ask for help.

I CAN do things that make me happy.

I CAN do things that keep me safe.

I CAN see that I am not alone.

I CAN remain in control of myself.

I always have control over myself. I CAN be responsible.

I CAN handle change.

I CAN stay in control.

I WILL.

Humor

In the space below, draw, write, or paste pictures of things that make you smile and laugh.

Assertiveness

I can stand up for myself by using my words to get what I need and want.

I can be respectful and use an "I" message.

"I feel hungry. I would like a snack please."
"I feel lonely. I would like to call my friend please."
"No, thank you. I do not want to do that. Instead, let's
_____."

I can think of more ways to be assertive. "I" messages that I can use are:

_____

_____

_____

_____

_____

_____

_____

_____

_____

Thinking and Acting

Positive thoughts lead to positive actions.

What are some positive things I can think and do to help me see things in a positive way?

Example: My friend is mean to me at school.

Positive Thoughts: We have been friends for a long time and have been through this before. I know we will be fine. I am hanging with my other friend today anyway. When my friend is ready to talk, I can talk about how I feel and how I want to be treated by being assertive.

A positive statement or two that I can say to myself:

_____

_____

_____

_____

_____

_____

_____

_____

_____

Plenty of Activities

Activities that make me feel happy can help me cope. I can use these fun things to stay in control.

Some ideas for me might be (circle the ones you think will help you)

talking to someone I trust
going for a walk
playing sports
doing a craft
listening to music
reading
building with blocks
playing with my friends
journaling my thoughts and feelings
relaxing each muscle

riding a bike
playing with my pet
squeezing a ball or a pillow
running
thinking of something happy
playing video games
deep breathing
dancing a silly dance
counting to one hundred

There are more activities that make coping with feelings and situations easier. Here are some that I think will help me:

_____

_____

_____

_____

_____

_____

_____

Appendix C

Anger Management

Everyone gets angry. Anger, frustration, and all other feelings are normal human reactions. Feeling angry is okay.

Simply saying "Feeling angry is okay, but it is not okay to hit, kick, yell, or [insert behavior]. Let's practice some ways to help us feel better when we are angry" is a great place to start the learning process with your children.

Stop, Think, Go

The Stop, Think, Go method teaches self-control and positive decision-making. Follow these steps to teach and practice this skill when your child is calm. That will make managing anger with this method more successful.

With practice and consistency, these steps will become automatic for your child. The result will be your child being able to independently control their decisions and to return to a calm state.

1. *Stop.* Show your child how to take slow deep breaths. Advise them to breathe in to the count of three, hold it to the count of three, and exhale to the count of three. Repeat these steps until they feel calm.

   It also helps to have your child visualize a relaxing place. Have them think of the sights, sounds, and smells of the chosen place as they close their eyes and begin to relax.

2. *Think.* Encourage them to think about their choices. Help them to select which one is the best choice.

   When creating independence with this skill, help your children weigh out the positive and negative consequences associated with their choices.

   Use scenarios such as these to help practice this skill.

   - Alex feels angry because his mother will not let him watch another television show. What are some choices that he has? What are the consequences to each of those choices? What should Alex do? Why?
   - Samantha is angry because her friend told others Samantha's biggest secret. What are some choices that she has? What are the consequences to each of those choices? What should Samantha do? Why?

3. *Go.* Tell your child to choose the best choice. If it turns out that it is not the best choice after all, try another.

Make copies of the "I Can Solve This Problem!" form found in this appendix. I recommend that you and your child use this form with made-up scenarios before using it in real situations to increase the effectiveness of the intervention. That way, you both get comfortable with seeing how to find calmness and how to use positive problem-solving.

Allow your child to use this to guide them during times of frustration all the way to times of extreme anger. Be ready with praise for any steps taken in the right direction, even if these steps weren't done independently

Managing one's own emotions is a difficult task to master. Be patient and consistent. The payoffs for you and your child will be great!

Problem-Solving Steps

1. What is the problem?
2. Think of at least two ways to solve the problem
3. Choose one way
4. Try your choice
5. Did your choice solve the problem?
6. If you answered, "No" to step five, try your second choice to solve the problem

I Can Solve This Problem!
Do This Now!

1. Close my eyes.
2. Count to ten.
3. Think of a happy place or time. See it, smell it, hear it.
4. Take five deep, slow breaths.
5. Repeat.

This is a picture of how I feel

Right now I feel _____

_____

I feel this way because_____

_____

_____

_____

These are my choices: This is what might happen:

_____   _____

_____   _____

_____   _____

_____   _____

I will pick _____ to solve my problem.
If it does not work, I will pick _____.

What Is Your Body Telling You?

Anger is a normal emotion.

Knowing your physical signs of frustration and anger can improve your awareness of negative feelings and help you to manage emotions before they get out of control.

Use the image below to identify areas of your body that signal that you may become angry. Common areas include sweaty palms, a racing heart, a nervous stomach, and a clenched jaw, to name a few.

Listening to your body will help to identify your triggers to anger. Once your triggers are identified, use the problem-solving steps (stop, think, go) to decide what you can do to head off anger before it starts.

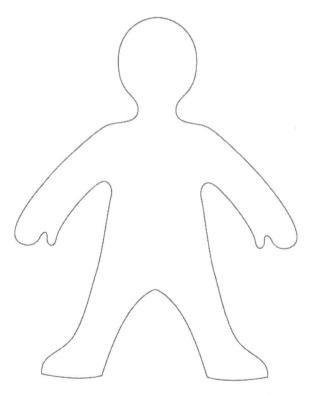

Positive Thoughts, Positive Actions

Positive self-talk is a fancy way of giving yourself a pep talk through phrases such as

"I can do this!"

"I have been through this before and everything turned out fine. I know I can get through it again."

"I am strong."

"There are a lot of people who care about me. I can ask someone for help if I need it."

"I have a lot to be thankful for in my life."

"This situation is temporary."

"There is nothing to fear."

Statements like the ones listed here give people hope, strength, and courage to face life's difficult situations.

List a few phrases that help you to feel confident.

_____

_____

_____

_____

_____

_____

Assertiveness

Assertiveness is a lifelong skill that is needed at all stages of development.

Below you will find "I" message examples. These are statements that we make in order to respectfully get our needs and wants met.

Print these cards out for easy use when practicing how to use "I" messages. Keep some in the car, in your backpack, in your room, or any other place that will help remind you of how to be assertive.

I feel _____

when _____

I want _____

I feel _____

when _____

I want _____

I feel _____

when _____

I want _____

I feel _____

when _____

I want _____

Appendix D

Social Skills

This Is Being Social

- You and your peers smile at one another as you pass in the hallway.
- You notice that someone is crying and you ask if they need help.
- A peer unknowingly drops money. You pick it up and give it back to them.
- Someone says excuse me when they pass by.
- When becoming upset with someone, you choose to walk away instead of yelling at them
- When speaking, you use eye contact and inquire into the listener's thoughts and feelings.
- A friend invited someone that you don't get along with to their party. You decide to go anyway and treat everyone with respect.

Those life experiences describe a lot of what it means to use social skills. I could go on and on, but I think you get the idea. Possessing strong social skills is a huge predictor of life success. Whether your child is lacking in the social skill department due to absence of appropriate exposure, a disability, or they are just taking their sweet time in making gains in this area, now is the time to address their need.

Social skills should be spoken about and practiced with your children regularly. Even more importantly, by using appropriate social skills consistently in your daily life, you are being a positive example to your children. Children learn best by observing and repeating what they see their parents and other respected individuals do. Do your best to talk about, practice, and regularly demonstrate social skills during each and every day. The following are just a few of the social skills that your child should possess and use regularly:

- Be courteous
- Show empathy
- Have anger management skills
- Know how to cope
- Communicate with others using verbal (their words) and nonverbal (body language) means
- Know how to solve problems by using their words
- Be able to deal with disappointment in age-appropriate ways
- Cooperate with others
- Show integrity

Some of these skills are so important that they should be incorporated into regular discussions and practice. Teaching your children social skills that include the important aspects of empathy for others, coping skills, problem-solving skills, and integrity should be incorporated into daily interactions. Decide on a skill for the week and practice at every opportunity. Be very careful to always use the skill yourself even if your think your child is not around. Being a positive role model will have the greatest impact.

If you struggle with teaching and practicing social skills with your children, attend family counseling or enroll them in group counseling with other peers. Just as previously listed, you must also use the skills that are being/have been taught. To do this, speak with your child's counselor so the skills from counseling can be carried over to daily life.

To get started, take a look at the following ideas. Each one gives you a powerful way in which to engage your children in learning about social skills. You may find that certain ones will work perfectly for your child, while others may serve to give you an idea of how to regularly incorporate the skill. Regardless of what works best for your family, be sure to always use the foundations to positive parenting found in the first five chapters. Having a strong foundation in place while teaching skills will result in greater results.

Get 'em All

The word "all" in the heading refers to all the social skills listed above and to all ages of children. How could this be? Let me tell you. At some point throughout each day, children of all ages engage in activities where they are either directly involved socially or are observing social interactions. Think about it:

- When we watch television, we see social interactions.
- When video games are played, the characters interact with others and/or with things.
- Children go to school, which is a very social place.
- Going to a holiday or birthday party is an obvious social event.
- When reading a book, the characters or theme will generally have a social dynamic.
- Interacting with family members is a social act.
- Reading or listening to the news speaks to the world's social aspects.

Use these times, plus other experiences that your children are exposed to, as a learning tool to reflect upon social skills. This is easy. There is no planning. Just take what life gives you!

For example, as you and your child view a social interaction, ask them the following questions:

- What do you think about what you saw?
- What would you have done differently?
- What would you have done the same?
- How would you feel in that situation?
- How would others feel?

Answering these questions gets them thinking about how their choices affect their own feelings and also the feelings of others. They also learn that appropriate social skills will not only bring acceptance but success too.

Follow these same guidelines for all the other social exposure areas that occur each day. Bringing these things to the attention of your children in a positive way allows for growth in the understanding of social skills along with a further comfort level in communicating openly with you about life choices. This is a win-win for everyone involved!

Role-Playing

In addition to the "get 'em all" activities listed above, role-playing has the power to teach endless social skills; it also meets children's needs of all ages. Role-playing consists of each of you taking on a role and staying in character while acting out a situation.

Consider the current needs of your children when selecting topics for role-playing scenarios. Invite the whole family to participate. Each family member should take turns picking a folded piece of paper and reading the situation to the group. The person that picked the paper takes the lead role and picks family members for the remaining roles.

When acting out each scenario, the characters need to demonstrate appropriate social skills. It is tempting for children to want to act in an inappropriate way to be funny. However, allowing them to have fun while being inappropriate sends the wrong message.

Role-playing appropriate social skills can be just as fun. Once all the situations have been acted out, ask your children to verbalize what they learned from this activity and allow them to pick a special snack or prize for using appropriate social skills.

Tap into Your Artsy Side

Most children love to do arts and crafts; this is especially true for primary-age children. As they grow, children who have an interest in art begin to refine their skills as artists. The creativity of a child is to be admired!

Tap into this existing resource by getting poster board, paint, construction paper, markers, crayons, stickers, and other art supplies that are of interest to your children. Have some fun together creating items that show age-appropriate social skills. Some ideas include the following:

- Make puppets to be used during role-playing.
- Create a poster to hang in your child's room.
- Create a social skills collage for the whole family to see.
- Use clay to construct people using social skills.
- Put together a paper chain where each link contains one way in which your child will show social skills.

Calling All Authors

Creativity can easily extend beyond arts and crafts activities. Many kids express themselves through writing. If this describes your child, challenge them to write a story about social skills. You can then look into getting it published in the school newsletter or local paper.

If your child is into illustrations for written work, ask them to draw social skills in a comic strip format, or pretend that their pictures will tell a story on their own in an art gallery. (This gallery can be placed on one of your walls at home for all to see.)

Online Media

When you do a search on values, integrity, morals, and of course, social skills, you are sure to find information, clips, and resources that will engage children in this topic.

Depending on the age of your children, ask them to search these topics and to then show you their favorites. If your children are young, try to do some of the research on your own and then show them what you found. When looking at online media, use the ideas listed previously to encourage your children to explore the positive and negative social characteristics that they saw. Try your best to urge your children to practice social skills by replicating viewed positive skills along with correcting any negative social interactions that apply to your child's functioning.

Be a Spy

Once a particular social skill has been identified, discussed, and practiced at home, take your child to a public place to observe others. See how many times you and your child can find people showing the identified skill. Each time you do this activity, estimate how many times you and your child think the skill will be seen. Try to beat this number by working together and by being super spies!

Weekly Social Bonus

Use the established behavior plan to enhance social skills. Now, before you worry about how you will have to change things up, let me assure you that this is an easy (and fun) addition. Yes that is right; it is an addition, not a change.

Along with your goals and incentives, provide a bonus to your child each time they demonstrate the social skill of the week. Once you and your child have talked about the skill and practiced the skill, allow them to see that they can now earn even more positive incentives by using the social skills while trying to meet their goals. This is like extra credit! Everyone likes extra credit, and your child will be excited to earn even more positive recognition for you.

Make it Fun

I have seen countless children who have had fun with each of the activities listed in this section. This is especially true when their parents put the time and energy into making them as fun as possible.

If your family is looking for even more fun, consider playing a game of social skills charades, find board games that focus on social skills, go out in public while practicing an identified social skill, or play invented games such as having to describe a social skill to other people for them to guess. The choices are truly endless!

Appendix E

Discipline vs. Punishment Checklist

Use this tool to identify ways in which you are using a discipline and/or a punishment approach to raising your children. Each time you use this checklist, reflect on what you can do to further promote supportive teaching rather than punishment.

Discipline

☐ Discipline happens over time to help children hear, see, and perform appropriate behaviors.

☐ Discipline teaches children right from wrong in loving, patient, caring, and positive ways.

☐ Discipline helps to improve children's self-esteem and sense of belonging to their family and to this world by giving them opportunities to experience success.

☐ Discipline gives positive reinforcement for all the right choices children make.

☐ Parents who use discipline take the time to talk with their children, answer their questions, show them right from wrong, and allow for compromise.

Punishment

- ☐ Punishment does not teach right from wrong.
- ☐ Punishment is essentially negative as it involves people in authority (parents) asserting power and control over others (children).
- ☐ Parenting methods that rely on control over children only results in greater misbehavior because children end up seeking more control over their lives and attempt to make choices out of rebellion.
- ☐ Punishment rarely includes time taken to explain things to children or to show them what is acceptable. Punishment for actions without an explanation of why does no good in changing behavior.
- ☐ Punishment does not work to get rid of misbehavior.

Appendix F

Consequence Checklist

Use this checklist to assist you in selecting and evaluating the consequences that are set for your children. Remember that the goal of setting up consequences is to allow your children to learn from their actions given consistent and appropriate consequences. Follow these guidelines and you can't go wrong.

- ☐ The consequence is directly linked to my child's behavior.
- ☐ The consequence is given immediately or as soon as possible after the behavior.
- ☐ The consequence is given each time the behavior is used.
- ☐ The consequence is developmentally appropriate for my child.
- ☐ The consequence is not too severe or too mild to convey understanding.
- ☐ The consequence is used to positively teach my child about appropriate behavior.
- ☐ Negative and logical consequences are given with as much privacy as possible.
- ☐ The consequence is given in an environment that has little to no distractions when possible.
- ☐ Negative and logical consequences are given in a respectful manner, void of put downs, yelling, hitting, and name-calling.
- ☐ Negative and logical consequences are given in a calm manner.

□ A brief discussion takes place regarding how consequences and appropriate behaviors apply to current childhood issues as well as how they will apply when my child is an adult.

□ My child knew of the positive or negative consequence prior to it being given.

□ My child is able to tell me what they did to earn the consequence given.

□ When a negative or logical consequence is given, my child can tell me the choices available for improving future behavior.

Index

Reference

American Psychiatric Association. (2013). Diagnostic and statistical manual of mental disorders (5th ed.). Washington, DC.

Credits

Visual behavior plan:
<a href='http://www.123rf.com/photo_17789193_bully.html'>twindesign / 123RF Stock Photo</a>

<a href='http://www.123rf.com/photo_9824771_child-with-gymnastic-ball-on-bleu-studio-background.html'>alenkasm/ 123RF Stock Photo</a>

<a href='http://www.123rf.com/photo_7019953_studio-shot-of-screaming-boy.html'>jirkaejc / 123RF Stock Photo</a>

<a href='http://www.123rf.com/photo_14722096_chocolate-cookies.html'>lindwa / 123RF Stock Photo</a>

<a href='http://www.123rf.com/photo_347267_little-girl-helping-to-clean-the-house.html'>barsik / 123RF Stock Photo</a>

Image credit: <a href='http://www.123rf.com/photo_14212489_